THE BIBLE

TRUTH MATTERS!

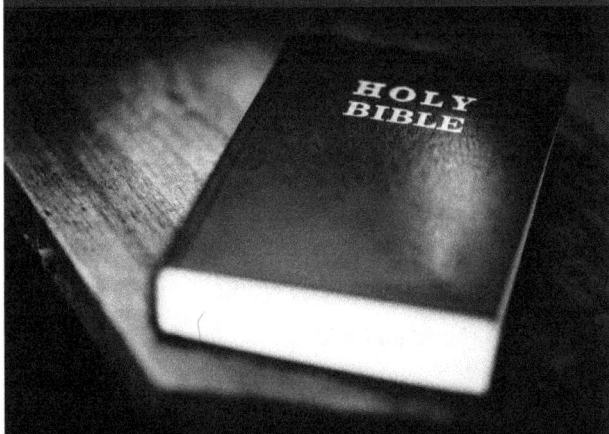

EDWARD D. ANDREWS

GOD'S WORD

THE BIBLE

God's Word

Edward D. Andrews

Christian Publishing House
Cambridge, Ohio

Christian Publishing House
Professional Conservative Christian
Publishing of the Good News!

CPH Since 2005

Unless otherwise indicated, Scripture quotations are from the Updated American Standard Version of the Holy Scriptures, 2016 edition (UASV).

THE BIBLE: God's Word

Authored by Edward D. Andrews

ISBN-13: **978-1-945757-53-2**

ISBN-10: **1-945757-53-1**

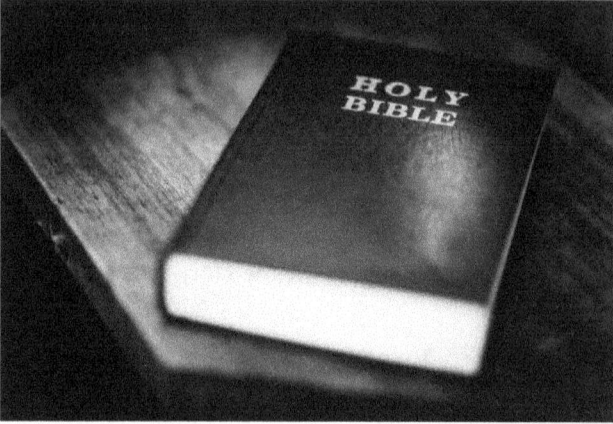

Table of Contents

CHAPTER 1 The Revelation of God..............1

Review Questions...28

CHAPTER 2 Inspiration and Inerrancy in the Writing Process 30

Review Questions...72

CHAPTER 3 Inerrancy................................ 73

Review Questions... 81

CHAPTER 4 Canonicity of the Bible 82

Review Questions..................................... 120

CHAPTER 5 Clarity of Scripture 122

Review Questions.....................................137

Bibliography..139

CHAPTER 1 The Revelation of God

By Benjamin B. Warfield

I. The Nature of Revelation.

1. The Religion of the Bible the Only Supernatural Religion:

The religion of the Bible is a frankly supernatural religion. By this is not meant merely that, according to it, all men, as creatures, live, move and have their being in God. It is meant that, according to it, God has intervened extraordinarily, in the course of the sinful world's development, for the salvation of men otherwise lost. In Eden the Lord God had been present with sinless man in such a sense as to form a distinct element in his social environment (Gen. 3:8). This intimate association was broken up by the Fall. But God did not therefore withdraw Himself from concernment with men. Rather, He began at once a series of interventions in human history by means of which man might be rescued from his sin and, despite it, brought to the end destined for him. These interventions involved the segregation of a people for Himself, by whom God should be known, and whose distinction should be that God should be "nigh unto them" as He was not to other nations (De 4:7; Ps 145:18). But this people was not permitted to imagine that it owed its segregation to anything in itself fitted to attract or determine the Divine preference; no consciousness was more poignant in Israel than that Yahweh had chosen it, not it Him, and that Yahweh's choice of it rested solely on His gracious will. Nor was this people permitted to imagine that it was for its own sake alone that it had been singled out to be the sole recipient of the knowledge of Yahweh; it was made clear from the beginning that God's mysteriously gracious dealing with it had as its ultimate end the blessing of the whole world (Gen. 12:2-; 17:4-6, 16; 18:18; 22:18; compare Ro 4:13), the bringing together again of the divided families of the earth under the glorious reign of Yahweh, and the reversal of the curse under which the whole world lay for its sin (Ge 12:3). Meanwhile, however, Yahweh was known only in Israel. To Israel God showed His word and made known His statutes and judgments, and after this fashion He dealt with no other nation; and therefore none other knew His judgments (Ps 147:19). Accordingly, when the hope of Israel (who was also the

1

desire of all nations) came, His own lips unhesitatingly declared that the salvation He brought, though of universal application, was "from the Jews" (Joh 4:22). And the nations to which this salvation had not been made known are declared by the chief agent in its proclamation to them to be, meanwhile, "far off," "having no hope" and "without God in the world" (Eph 2:12), because they were aliens from the commonwealth of Israel and strangers from the covenant of the promise.

The religion of the Bible, thus announces itself, not as the product of men's search after God, if haply they may feel after Him and find Him, but as the creation in men of the gracious God, forming a people for Himself, that they may show forth His praise. In other words, the religion of the Bible presents itself as distinctively a revealed religion. Or rather, to speak more exactly, it announces itself as the revealed religion, as the only revealed religion; and sets itself as such over against all other religions, which are represented as all products, in a sense in which it is not, of the art and device of man.

It is not, however, implied in this exclusive claim to revelation--which is made by the religion of the Bible in all the stages of its history--that the living God, who made the heaven and the earth and the sea and all that in them is, has left Himself without witness among the peoples of the world (Ac 14:17). It is asserted indeed, that in the process of His redemptive work, God suffered for a season all the nations to walk in their own ways; but it is added that to none of them has He failed to do good, and to give from heaven rains and fruitful seasons, filling their hearts with food and gladness. And not only is He represented as thus constantly showing Himself in His providence not far from any one of them, thus wooing them to seek Him if haply they might feel after Him and find Him (Ac 17:27), but as from the foundation of the world openly manifesting Himself to them in the works of His hands, in which His everlasting power and divinity are clearly seen (Ro 1:20). That men at large have not retained Him in their knowledge, or served Him as they ought, is not due therefore to failure on His part to keep open the way to knowledge of Him, but to the darkening of their senseless hearts by sin and to the vanity of their sin-deflected reasonings (Ro 1:21ff), by means of which they have supplanted the truth of God by a lie and have come to worship and serve the creature rather

2

than the ever-blessed Creator. It is, indeed, precisely because in their sin they have thus held down the truth in unrighteousness and have refused to have God in their knowledge (so it is intimated); and because, moreover, in their sin, the revelation God gives of Himself in His works of creation and providence no longer suffices for men's needs, that God has intervened supernaturally in the course of history to form a people for Himself, through whom at length all the world should be blessed.

2. General and Special Revelation:

It is quite obvious that there are brought before us in these several representations two species or stages of revelation, which should be discriminated to avoid confusion. There is the revelation which God continuously makes to all men: by it His power and divinity are made known. And there is the revelation which He makes exclusively to His chosen people: through it His saving grace is made known. Both species or stages of revelation are insisted upon throughout the Scriptures. They are, for example, brought significantly together in such a declaration as we find in Ps 19:1-14: "The heavens declare the glory of God .... their line is gone out through all the earth" (Ps 19:1, 4); "The law of Yahweh is perfect, restoring the soul" (Ps 19:7). The Psalmist takes his beginning here from the praise of the glory of God, the Creator of all that is, which has been written upon the very heavens, that none may fail to see it. From this he rises, however, quickly to the more full-throated praise of the mercy of Yahweh, the covenant God, who has visited His people with saving instruction. Upon this higher revelation there is finally based a prayer for salvation from sin, which ends in a great threefold acclamation, instinct with adoring gratitude: "O Yahweh, my rock, and my redeemer" (Ps 19:14). "The heavens," comments Lord Bacon, "indeed tell of the glory of God, but not of His will according to which the poet prays to be pardoned and sanctified." In so commenting, Lord Bacon touches the exact point of distinction between the two species or stages of revelation. The one is adapted to man as man; the other to man as sinner; and since man, on becoming sinner, has not ceased to be man, but has only acquired new needs requiring additional provisions to bring him to the end of his existence, so the revelation directed to man as sinner does not supersede that given to man as man, but supplements it with these new provisions for his attainment,

3

in his new condition of blindness, helplessness and guilt induced by sin, of the end of his being.

These two species or stages of revelation have been commonly distinguished from one another by the distinctive names of natural and supernatural revelation, or general and special revelation, or natural and soteriological revelation. Each of these modes of discriminating them has its particular fitness and describes a real difference between the two in nature, reach or purpose. The one is communicated through the media of natural phenomena, occurring in the course of nature or of history; the other implies an intervention in the natural course of things and is not merely in source but in mode supernatural. The one is addressed generally to all intelligent creatures, and is therefore accessible to all men; the other is addressed to a special class of sinners, to whom God would make known His salvation. The one has in view to meet and supply the natural need of creatures for knowledge of their God; the other to rescue broken and deformed sinners from their sin and its consequences. But, though thus distinguished from one another, it is important that the two species or stages of revelation should not be set in opposition to one another, or the closeness of their mutual relations or the constancy of their interaction be obscured. They constitute together a unitary whole, and each is incomplete without the other. In its most general idea, revelation is rooted in creation and the relations with His intelligent creatures into which God has brought Himself by giving them being. Its object is to realize the end of man's creation, to be attained only through knowledge of God and perfect and unbroken communion with Him. On the entrance of sin into the world, destroying this communion with God and obscuring the knowledge of Him derived from nature, another mode of revelation was necessitated, having also another content, adapted to the new relation to God and the new conditions of intellect, heart and will brought about by sin. It must not be supposed, however, that this new mode of revelation was an ex post facto expedient, introduced to meet an unforeseen contingency. The actual course of human development was in the nature of the case the expected and the intended course of human development, for which man was created; and revelation, therefore, in its double form was the divine purpose for man from the beginning, and constitutes a unitary provision for the realization of the end of his creation in the actual circumstances in which he exists. We may distinguish in this unitary revelation the two elements by the cooperation of which the effect is produced; but we should bear in mind that only by their cooperation is the effect produced. Without special revelation, general revelation would be for sinful men incomplete and ineffective, and could issue, as in point of fact it has issued wherever it alone has been accessible, only in leaving them without excuse (Ro 1:20). Without general revelation, special revelation would lack that basis in the fundamental knowledge of God as the mighty and wise, righteous and good maker and ruler of all things, apart from which the further revelation of this great God's interventions in the world for the salvation of sinners could not be either intelligible, credible or operative.

(1) Revelation in Eden.

Only in Eden has general revelation been adequate to the needs of man. Not being a sinner, man in Eden had no need of that grace of God itself by which sinners are restored to communion with Him, or of the special revelation of this grace of God to sinners to enable them to live with God. And not being a sinner, man in Eden, as he contemplated the works of God, saw God in the unclouded mirror of his mind with a clarity of vision, and lived with Him in the untroubled depths of his heart with a trustful intimacy of association, inconceivable to sinners. Nevertheless, the revelation of God in Eden was not merely "natural." Not only does the prohibition of the forbidden fruit involve a positive commandment (Ge 2:16), but the whole history implies an immediacy of intercourse with God which cannot easily be set to the credit of the picturesque art of the narrative, or be fully accounted for by the vividness of the perception of God in His works proper to sinless creatures. The impression is strong that what is meant to be conveyed to us is that man dwelt with God in Eden, and enjoyed with Him immediate and not merely mediate communion. In that case, we may understand that if man had not fallen, he would have continued to enjoy immediate intercourse with God, and that the cessation of this immediate intercourse is due to sin. It is not then the supernaturalness of special revelation which is rooted in sin, but, if we may be allowed the expression, the specialness of supernatural revelation. Had man not fallen, heaven would have continued to lie about him through all his history, as it lay about his infancy; every man would have enjoyed direct vision of God and immediate speech with Him. Man having fallen, the cherubim and the flame of a sword, turning every way, keep the path; and God breaks His way in a round-about fashion into man's darkened heart to reveal there His redemptive love. By slow steps and gradual stages He at once works out His saving purpose and molds the world for its reception, choosing a people for Himself and training it through long and weary ages, until at last when the fullness of time has come, He bares His arm and sends out the proclamation of His great salvation to all the earth.

(2) Revelation among the Heathen.

Certainly, from the gate of Eden onward, God's general revelation ceased to be, in the strict sense, supernatural. It is, of course, not meant that God deserted His world and left it to fester in its iniquity. His providence still ruled over all, leading steadily onward to the goal for which man had been created, and of the attainment of which in God's own good time and way the very continuance of men's existence, under God's providential government, was a pledge. And His Spirit still everywhere wrought upon the hearts of men, stirring up all their powers (though created in the image of God, marred and impaired by sin) to their best activities, and to such splendid effect in every department of human achievement as to command the admiration of all ages, and in the highest region of all, that of conduct, to call out from an apostle the encomium that though they had no law they did by nature (observe the word "nature") the things of the law. All this, however, remains within the limits of Nature, that is to say, within the sphere of operation of divinely-directed and assisted second causes. It illustrates merely the heights to which the powers of man may attain under the guidance of providence and the influences of what we have learned to call God's "common grace." Nowhere, throughout the whole ethnic domain, are the conceptions of God and His ways put within the reach of man, through God's revelation of Himself in the works of creation and providence, transcended; nowhere is the slightest knowledge betrayed of anything concerning God and His purposes, which could be known only by its being supernaturally told to men. Of the entire body of "saving truth," for example, which is the burden of what we call "special

6

revelation," the whole heathen world remained in total ignorance. And even its hold on the general truths of religion, not being vitalized by supernatural enforcements, grew weak, and its knowledge of the very nature of God decayed, until it ran out to the dreadful issue which Paul sketches for us in that inspired philosophy of religion which he incorporates in the latter part of the first chapter of the Epistle to the Romans.

Behind even the ethnic development, there lay, of course, the supernatural intercourse of man with God which had obtained before the entrance of sin into the world, and the supernatural revelations at the gate of Eden (Gen. 3:8), and at the second origin of the human race, the Flood (Gen. 8:21-22; 9:1-17). How long the tradition of this primitive revelation lingered in nooks and corners of the heathen world, conditioning and vitalizing the natural revelation of God always accessible, we have no means of estimating. Neither is it easy to measure the effect of God's special revelation of Himself to His people upon men outside the bounds of, indeed, but coming into contact with, this chosen people, or sharing with them a common natural inheritance. Lot and Ishmael and Esau can scarcely have been wholly ignorant of the word of God which came to Abraham and Isaac and Jacob; nor could the Egyptians from whose hands God wrested His people with a mighty arm fail to learn something of Yahweh, any more than the mixed multitudes who witnessed the ministry of Christ could fail to infer something from His gracious walk and mighty works. It is natural to infer that no nation which was intimately associated with Israel's life could remain entirely unaffected by Israel's revelation. But whatever impressions were thus conveyed reached apparently individuals only: the heathen which surrounded Israel, even those most closely affiliated with Israel, remained heathen; they had no revelation. In the sporadic instances when God visited an alien with a supernatural communication--such as the dreams sent to Abimelech (Gen 20:1-18) and to Pharaoh (Ge 40:1-23; 41:1-57) and to Nebuchadnezzar (Da 2:1ff) and to the soldier in the camp of Midian (Jg 7:13)--it was in the interests, not of the heathen world, but of the chosen people that they were sent; and these instances derive their significance wholly from this fact. There remain, no doubt, the mysterious figure of Melchizedek, perhaps also of Jethro, and the strange apparition of Balaam, who also, however, appear in the sacred narrative only in connection with the history of God's dealings with His people and in their interest. Their unexplained appearance cannot in any event avail to modify the general fact that the life of the heathen peoples lay outside the supernatural revelation of God. The heathen were suffered to walk in their own ways (Ac 14:16).

II. The Process of Revelation.

Meanwhile, however, God had not forgotten them, but was preparing salvation for them also through the supernatural revelation of His grace that He was making to His people. According to the Biblical representation, in the midst of and working confluently with the revelation which He has always been giving of Himself on the plane of Nature, God was making also from the very fall of man a further revelation of Himself on the plane of grace. In contrast with His general, natural revelation, in which all men by virtue of their very nature as men share, this special, supernatural revelation was granted at first only to individuals, then progressively to a family, a tribe, a nation, a race, until, when the fullness of time was come, it was made the possession of the whole world. It may be difficult to obtain from Scripture a clear account of why God chose thus to give this revelation of His grace only progressively; or, to be more explicit, through the process of a historical development. Such is, however, the ordinary mode of the Divine working: it is so that God made the worlds, it is so that He creates the human race itself, the recipient of this revelation, it is so that He builds up His kingdom in the world and in the individual soul, which only gradually comes whether to the knowledge of God or to the fruition of His salvation. As to the fact, the Scriptures are explicit, tracing for us, or rather embodying in their own growth, the record of the steady advance of this gracious revelation through definite stages from its first faint beginnings to its glorious completion in Jesus Christ.

1. Place of Revelation among the Redemptive Acts of God:

So express is its relation to the development of the kingdom of God itself, or rather to that great series of divine operations which are directed to the building up of the kingdom of God in the world, that it is sometimes confounded with them or thought of as simply their reflection in the contemplating mind of man.

Thus it is not infrequently said that revelation, meaning this special redemptive revelation, has been communicated in deeds, not in words; and it is occasionally elaborately argued that the sole manner in which God has revealed Himself as the Saviour of sinners is just by performing those mighty acts by which sinners are saved. This is not, however, the Biblical representation. Revelation is, of course, often made through the instrumentality of deeds; and the series of His great redemptive acts by which He saves the world constitutes the pre-eminent revelation of the grace of God--so far as these redemptive acts are open to observation and are perceived in their significance. But revelation, after all, is the correlate of understanding and has as its proximate end just the production of knowledge, though not, of course, knowledge for its own sake, but for the sake of salvation. The series of the redemptive acts of God, accordingly, can properly be designated "revelation" only when and so far as they are contemplated as adapted and designed to produce knowledge of God and His purpose and methods of grace. No bare series of unexplained acts can be thought, however, adapted to produce knowledge, especially if these acts be, as in this case, of a highly transcendental character. Nor can this particular series of acts be thought to have as its main design the production of knowledge; its main design is rather to save man. No doubt the production of knowledge of the divine grace is one of the means by which this main design of the redemptive acts of God is attained. But this only renders it the more necessary that the proximate result of producing knowledge should not fail; and it is doubtless for this reason that the series of redemptive acts of God has not been left to explain itself, but the explanatory word has been added to it. Revelation thus appears, however, not as the mere reflection of the redeeming acts of God in the minds of men, but as a factor in the redeeming work of God, a component part of the series of His redeeming acts, without which that series would be incomplete and so far inoperative for its main end. Thus, the Scriptures represent it, not confounding revelation with the series of the redemptive acts of God, but placing it among the redemptive acts of God and giving it a function as a substantive element in the operations by which the merciful God saves sinful men. It is therefore not made even a mere constant accompaniment of the redemptive acts of God, giving their explanation that they may be understood. It occupies a far more independent place among them than this, and as frequently precedes them to prepare their way as it accompanies or follows them to interpret their meaning. It is, in one word, itself a redemptive act of God and by no means the least important in the series of His redemptive acts.

This might, indeed, have been inferred from its very nature, and from the nature of the salvation which was being worked out by these redemptive acts of God. One of the most grievous of the effects of sin is the deformation of the image of God reflected in the human mind, and there can be no recovery from sin which does not bring with it the correction of this deformation and the reflection in the soul of man of the whole glory of the Lord God Almighty. Man is an intelligent being; his superiority over the brute is found, among other things, precisely in the direction of all his life by his intelligence; and his blessedness is rooted in the true knowledge of his God--for this is life eternal, that we should know the only true God and Him whom He has sent. Dealing with man as an intelligent being, God the Lord has saved him by means of a revelation, by which he has been brought into an evermore and more adequate knowledge of God, and been led ever more and more to do his part in working out his own salvation with fear and trembling as he perceived with ever more and more clearness how God is working it out for him through mighty deeds of grace.

2. Stages of Material Development:

This is not the place to trace, even in outline, from the material point of view, the development of God's redemptive revelation from its first beginnings, in the promise given to Abraham--or rather in what has been called the Protevangelium at the gate of Eden--to its completion in the advent and work of Christ and the teaching of His apostles; a steadily advancing development, which, as it lies spread out to view in the pages of Scripture, takes to those who look at it from the consummation backward, the appearance of the shadow cast athwart preceding ages by the great figure of Christ. Even from the formal point of view, however, there has been pointed out a progressive advance in the method of revelation, consonant with its advance in content, or rather with the advancing stages of the building up of the kingdom of God, to subserve which is the whole object of revelation. Three distinct steps in revelation have been discriminated from this point of view. They are distinguished precisely by the increasing independence of revelation of the deeds constituting the series of the redemptive acts of God, in which, nevertheless, all revelation is a substantial element. Discriminations like this must not be taken too absolutely; and in the present instance the chronological sequence cannot be pressed. But, with much interlacing, three generally successive stages of revelation may be recognized, producing periods at least characteristically of what we may somewhat conventionally call theophany, prophecy and inspiration. What may be somewhat indefinitely marked off as the Patriarchal age is characteristically "the period of Outward Manifestations, and Symbols, and Theophanies": during it "God spoke to men through their senses, in physical phenomena, as the burning bush, the cloudy pillar, or in sensuous forms, as men, angels, etc. ..... In the Prophetic age, on the contrary, the prevailing mode of revelation was by means of inward prophetic inspiration": God spoke to men characteristically by the movements of the Holy Spirit in their hearts. "Prevailingly, at any rate from Samuel downwards, the supernatural revelation was a revelation in the hearts of the foremost thinkers of the people, or, as we call it, prophetic inspiration, without the aid of external sensuous symbols of God" (A.B. Davidson, Old Testament Prophecy, 1903, p. 148; compare pp. 12-14, 145 ff). This internal method of revelation reaches its culmination in the New Testament period, which is preeminently the age of the Spirit. What is especially characteristic of this age is revelation through the medium of the written word, what may be called apostolic as distinguished from prophetic inspiration. The revealing Spirit speaks through chosen men as His organs, but through these organs in such a fashion that the most intimate processes of their souls become the instruments by means of which He speaks His mind. Thus, at all events there are brought clearly before us three well-marked modes of revelation, which we may perhaps designate respectively, not with perfect discrimination, it is true, but not misleadingly, (1) external manifestation, (2) internal suggestion, and (3) concursive operation.

III. The Modes of Revelation.

1. Modes of Revelation:

Theophany may be taken as the typical form of "external manifestation;" but by its side may be ranged all of those mighty works by which God makes Himself known, including express miracles, no doubt, but along with them every supernatural intervention in the affairs of men, by means of which a better understanding is communicated of what God is or what are His purposes of grace to a sinful race. Under "internal suggestion" may be subsumed all the characteristic phenomena of what is most properly spoken of as "prophecy": visions and dreams, which, according to a fundamental passage (Nu 12:6), constitute the typical forms of prophecy, and with them the whole "prophetic word," which shares its essential characteristic with visions and dreams, since it comes not by the will of man but from God. By "concursive operation" may be meant that form of revelation illustrated in an inspired psalm or epistle or history, in which no human activity--not even the control of the will--is superseded, but the Holy Spirit works in, with and through them all in such a manner as to communicate to the product qualities distinctly superhuman. There is no age in the history of the religion of the Bible, from that of Moses to that of Christ and His apostles, in which all these modes of revelation do not find place. One or another may seem particularly characteristic of this age or of that; but they all occur in every age. And they occur side by side, broadly speaking, on the same level. No discrimination is drawn between them in point of worthiness as modes of revelation, and much less in point of purity in the revelations communicated through them. The circumstance that God spoke to Moses, not by dream or vision but mouth to mouth, is, indeed, adverted to (Nu 12:8) as a proof of the peculiar favor shown to Moses and even of the superior dignity of Moses above other organs of revelation: God admitted him to an intimacy of intercourse which He did not accord to others. But though Moses was thus distinguished above all others in the dealings of God with him, no distinction is drawn between the revelations given through him and those given through other organs of revelation in point either of Divinity or of authority. And beyond this we have no Scriptural warrant to go on in contrasting one mode of revelation with another. Dreams may seem to us little fitted to serve as vehicles of divine communications. But there is no suggestion in Scripture that revelations through dreams stand on a lower plane than any others; and we should not fail to remember that the essential characteristics of revelations through dreams are shared by all forms of revelation in which (whether we should call them visions or not) the images or ideas which fill, or pass in procession through, the consciousness are determined by some other power than the recipient's own will. It may seem natural to suppose that revelations rise in rank in proportion to the fullness of the engagement of the mental activity of the recipient in their reception. But we should bear in mind that the intellectual or spiritual quality of a revelation is not derived from the recipient but from its Divine Giver. The fundamental fact in all revelation is that it is from God. This is what gives unity to the whole process of revelation, given though it may be in divers portions and in divers manners and distributed though it may be through the ages in accordance with the mere will of God, or as it may have suited His developing purpose--this and its unitary end, which is ever the building up of the kingdom of God. In whatever diversity of forms, by means of whatever variety of modes, in whatever distinguishable stages it is given, it is ever the revelation of the One God, and it is ever the one consistently developing redemptive revelation of God.

2. Equal Supernaturalness of the Several Modes:

On a prima facie view it may indeed seem likely that a difference in the quality of their supernaturalness would inevitably obtain between revelations given through such divergent modes. The completely supernatural character of revelations given in theophanies is obvious. He who will not allow that God speaks to man, to make known His gracious purposes toward him, has no other recourse here than to pronounce the stories legendary. The objectivity of the mode of communication which is adopted is intense, and it is thrown up to observation with the greatest emphasis. Into the natural life of man God intrudes in a purely supernatural manner, bearing a purely supernatural communication. In these communications we are given accordingly just a series of "naked messages of God." But not even in the Patriarchal age were all revelations given in theophanies or objective appearances. There were dreams, and visions, and revelations without explicit intimation in the narrative of how they were communicated. And when we pass on in the history, we do not, indeed, leave behind us theophanies and objective appearances. It is not only made the very characteristic of Moses, the greatest figure in the whole history of revelation except only that of Christ, that he knew God face to face (De 34:10), and God spoke to him mouth to mouth, even manifestly, and not in dark speeches (Nu 12:8); but throughout the whole history of revelation down to the appearance of Jesus to Paul on the road to Damascus, God has shown Himself visibly to His servants whenever it has seemed good to Him to do so and has spoken with them in objective speech. Nevertheless, it is expressly made the characteristic of the Prophetic age that God makes Himself known to His servants "in a vision," "in a dream" (Nu 12:6). And although, throughout its entire duration, God, in fulfillment of His promise (De 18:18), put His words in the mouths of His prophets and gave them His commandments to speak, yet it would seem inherent in the very employment of men as instruments of revelation that the words of God given through them are spoken by human mouths; and the purity of their supernaturalness may seem so far obscured. And when it is not merely the mouths of men with which God thus serves Himself in the delivery of His messages, but their minds and hearts as well--the play of their religious feelings, or the processes of their logical reasoning, or the tenacity of their memories, as, say, in a psalm or in an epistle, or a history--the supernatural element in the communication may easily seem to retire still farther into the background. It can scarcely be a matter of surprise, therefore, that question has been raised as to the relation of the natural and the supernatural in such revelations, and, in many current manners of thinking and speaking of them, the completeness of their supernaturalness has been limited and curtailed in the interests of the natural instrumentalities employed. The plausibility of such reasoning renders it the more necessary that we should observe the unvarying emphasis which the Scriptures place upon the absolute supernaturalness of revelation in all its modes alike. In the view of the Scriptures, the completely supernatural character of revelation is in no way lessened by the circumstance that it has been given through the instrumentality of men. They affirm, indeed, with the greatest possible emphasis that the Divine word delivered through men is the pure word of God, diluted with no human admixture whatever.

3. The Prophet God's Mouthpiece:

14

We have already been led to note that even on the occasion when Moses is exalted above all other organs of revelation (Nu 12:6 ff), in point of dignity and favor, no suggestion whatever is made of any inferiority, in either the directness or the purity of their supernaturalness, attaching to other organs of revelation. There might never afterward arise a prophet in Israel like unto Moses, whom the Lord knew face to face (Deut. 34:10). But each of the whole series of prophets raised up by Yahweh that the people might always know His will was to be like Moses in speaking to the people only what Yahweh commanded them (Deut. 18:15,18,20). In this great promise, securing to Israel the succession of prophets, there is also included a declaration of precisely how Yahweh would communicate His messages not so much to them as through them. "I will raise them up a prophet from among their brethren, like unto thee," we read (De 18:18), "and I will put my words in his mouth, and he shall speak unto them all that I shall command him." The process of revelation through the prophets was a process by which Yahweh put His words in the mouths of the prophets, and the prophets spoke precisely these words and no others. So the prophets themselves ever asserted. "Then Yahweh put forth his hand, and touched my mouth," explains Jeremiah in his account of how he received his prophecies, "and Yahweh said unto me, Behold, I have put my words in thy mouth" (Jer 1:9; compare Jer 5:14; Isa 51:16; 59:21; Num. 22:35; 23:5, 1216). Accordingly, the words "with which" they spoke were not their own but the Lord's: "And he said unto me," records Ezekiel, "Son of man, go, get thee unto the house of Israel, and speak with my words unto them" (Eze 3:4). It is a process of nothing other than "dictation" which is thus described (2Sa 14:3, 19), though, of course, the question may remain open of the exact processes by which this dictation is accomplished. The fundamental passage which brings the central fact before us in the most vivid manner is, no doubt, the account of the commissioning of Moses and Aaron given in Ex 4:10-17; 7:1-7. Here, in the most express words, Yahweh declares that He who made the mouth can be with it to teach it what to speak, and announces the precise function of a prophet to be that he is "a mouth of God," who speaks not his own but God's words. Accordingly, the Hebrew name for "prophet" (nabhi'), whatever may be its etymology, means throughout the Scriptures just "spokesman," though not "spokesman" in general, but Spokesman

15

by way of eminence, that is, God's spokesman; and the characteristic formula by which a prophetic declaration is announced is: "The word of Yahweh came to me," or the brief "saith Yahweh" (ne'um Yahweh). In no case does a prophet put his words forward as his own words. That he is a prophet at all is due not to choice on his own part, but to a call of God, obeyed often with reluctance; and he prophesies or forbears to prophesy, not according to his own will but as the Lord opens and shuts his mouth (Eze 3:26f) and creates for him the fruit of the lips (Isa 57:19; compare Isa 6:7; 50:4). In contrast with the false prophets, he strenuously asserts that he does not speak out of his own heart ("heart" in Biblical language includes the whole inner man), but all that he proclaims is the pure word of Yahweh.

4. Visionary Form of Prophecy:

The fundamental passage does not quite leave the matter, however, with this general declaration. It describes the characteristic manner in which Yahweh communicates His messages to His prophets as through the medium of visions and dreams. Neither visions in the technical sense of that word, nor dreams, appear, however, to have been the customary mode of revelation to the prophets, the record of whose revelations has come down to us. But, on the other hand, there are numerous indications in the record that the universal mode of revelation to them was one which was in some sense a vision, and can be classed only in the category distinctively so called.

The whole nomenclature of prophecy presupposes, indeed, its vision-form. Prophecy is distinctively a word, and what is delivered by the prophets is proclaimed as the "word of Yahweh." That it should be announced by the formula, "Thus saith the Lord," is, therefore, only what we expect; and we are prepared for such a description of its process as: "The Lord Yahweh .... wakeneth mine ear to hear," He "hath opened mine ear" (Isa 50:4-5). But this is not the way of speaking of their messages which is most usual in the prophets. Rather is the whole body of prophecy cursorily presented as a thing seen. Isaiah places at the head of his book: "The vision of Isaiah .... which he saw" (compare Isa 29:10-11; Ob 1:1); and then proceeds to set at the head of subordinate sections the remarkable words, "The word that Isaiah .... saw" (2:1); "the burden (margin "oracle") .... which

Isaiah .... did see" (13:1). Similarly there stand at the head of other prophecies: "the words of Amos .... which he saw" (Am 1:1); "the word of Yahweh that came to Micah .... which he saw" (Mic 1:1); "the oracle which Habakkuk the prophet did see" (Hab 1:1margin); and elsewhere such language occurs as this: "the word that Yahweh hath showed me" (Jer 38:21); "the prophets have seen .... oracles" (La 2:14); "the word of Yahweh came .... and I looked, and, behold" (Eze 1:3-4); "Woe unto the foolish prophets, that follow their own spirit, and have seen nothing" (Eze 13:3); "I .... will look forth to see what he will speak with me,.... Yahweh .... said, Write the vision" (Hab 2:1 f). It is an inadequate explanation of such language to suppose it merely a relic of a time when vision was more predominantly the form of revelation. There is no proof that vision in the technical sense ever was more predominantly the form of revelation than in the days of the great writing prophets; and such language as we have quoted too obviously represents the living point of view of the prophets to admit of the supposition that it was merely conventional on their lips. The prophets, in a word, represent the divine communications which they received as given to them in some sense in visions.

It is possible, no doubt, to exaggerate the significance of this. It is an exaggeration, for example, to insist that therefore all the divine communications made to the prophets must have come to them in external appearances and objective speech, addressed to and received by means of the bodily eye and ear. This would be to break down the distinction between manifestation and revelation, and to assimilate the mode of prophetic revelation to that granted to Moses, though these are expressly distinguished (Nu 12:6-8). It is also an exaggeration to insist that therefore the prophetic state must be conceived as that of strict ecstasy, involving the complete abeyance of all mental life on the part of the prophet (amentia), and possibly also accompanying physical effects. It is quite clear from the records which the prophets themselves give us of their revelations that their intelligence was alert in all stages of their reception of them. The purpose of both these extreme views is the good one of doing full justice to the objectivity of the revelations vouchsafed to the prophets. If these revelations took place entirely externally to the prophet, who merely stood off and contemplated them, or if they were

17

implanted in the prophets by a process so violent as not only to supersede their mental activity but, for the time being, to annihilate it, it would be quite clear that they came from a source other than the prophets' own minds. It is undoubtedly the fundamental contention of the prophets that the revelations given through them are not their own but wholly God's. The significant language we have just quoted from Eze 13:3: "Woe unto the foolish prophets, that follow their own spirit, and have seen nothing," is a typical utterance of their sense of the complete objectivity of their messages. What distinguishes the false prophets is precisely that they "prophesy out of their own heart" (Eze 13:2-17), or, to draw the antithesis sharply, that "they speak a vision of their own heart, and not out of the mouth of Yahweh" (Jer. 23:16, 26; 14:14). But these extreme views fail to do justice, the one to the equally important fact that the word of God, given through the prophets, comes as the pure and unmixed word of God not merely to, but from, the prophets; and the other to the equally obvious fact that the intelligence of the prophets is alert throughout the whole process of the reception and delivery of the revelation made through them.

That which gives to prophecy as a mode of revelation its place in the category of visions, strictly so called, and dreams is that it shares with them the distinguishing characteristic which determines the class. In them all alike the movements of the mind are determined by something extraneous to the subject's will, or rather, since we are speaking of supernaturally given dreams and visions, extraneous to the totality of the subject's own psychoses. A power not himself takes possession of his consciousness and determines it according to its will. That power, in the case of the prophets, was fully recognized and energetically asserted to be Yahweh Himself or, to be more specific, the Spirit of Yahweh (1Sa 10:6, 10; Ne 9:30; Zec 7:12; Joe 2:28-29). The prophets were therefore `men of the Spirit' (Ho 9:7). What constituted them prophets was that the Spirit was put upon them (Isa 42:1) or poured out on them (Joe 2:28-29), and they were consequently filled with the Spirit (Mic 3:8), or, in another but equivalent locution, that "the hand" of the Lord, or "the power of the hand" of the Lord, was upon them (2Ki 3:15; Eze 1:3; 3:14, 22; 33:22; 37:1; 40:1), that is to say, they were under the divine control. This control is represented as complete and compelling, so that, under it, the prophet becomes not the "mover," but the "moved" in the formation of his message. The apostle Peter very purely reflects the prophetic consciousness in his well-known declaration: `No prophecy of scripture comes of private interpretation; for prophecy was never brought by the will of man; but it was as borne by the Holy Spirit that men spoke from God' (2Pe 1:20-21).

5. "Passivity" of Prophets:

What this language of Peter emphasizes--and what is emphasized in the whole account which the prophets give of their own consciousness--is, to speak plainly, the passivity of the prophets with respect to the revelation given through them. This is the significance of the phrase: `it was as borne by the Holy Spirit that men spoke from God.' To be "borne" (pherein) is not the same as to be led (agein), much less to be guided or directed (hodegein): he that is "borne" contributes nothing to the movement induced, but is the object to be moved. The term "passivity" is, perhaps, however, liable to some misapprehension, and should not be overstrained. It is not intended to deny that the intelligence of the prophets was active in the reception of their message; it was by means of their active intelligence that their message was received: their intelligence was the instrument of revelation. It is intended to deny only that their intelligence was active in the production of their message: that it was creatively as distinguished from receptively active. For reception itself is a kind of activity. What the prophets are solicitous that their readers shall understand is that they are in no sense coauthors with God of their messages. Their messages are given them, given them entire, and given them precisely as they are given out by them. God speaks through them: they are not merely His messengers, but "His mouth." But at the same time their intelligence is active in the reception, retention and announcing of their messages, contributing nothing to them but presenting fit instruments for the communication of them-- instruments capable of understanding, responding profoundly to and zealously proclaiming them.

There is, no doubt, a not unnatural hesitancy abroad in thinking of the prophets as exhibiting only such merely receptive activities. In the interests of their personalities, we are asked not

19

to represent God as dealing mechanically with them, pouring His revelations into their souls to be simply received as in so many buckets, or violently wresting their minds from their own proper action that He may do His own thinking with them. Must we not rather suppose, we are asked, that all revelations must be "psychologically mediated," must be given "after the mode of moral mediation," and must be made first of all their recipients' "own spiritual possession"? And is not, in point of fact, the personality of each prophet clearly traceable in his message, and that to such an extent as to compel us to recognize him as in a true sense its real author? The plausibility of such questionings should not be permitted to obscure the fact that the mode of the communication of the prophetic messages which is suggested by them is directly contradicted by the prophets' own representations of their relations to the revealing Spirit. In the prophets' own view they were just instruments through whom God gave revelations which came from them, not as their own product, but as the pure word of Yahweh. Neither should the plausibility of such questionings blind us to their speciousness. They exploit subordinate considerations, which are not without their validity in their own place and under their own limiting conditions, as if they were the determining or even the sole considerations in the case, and in neglect of the really determining considerations. God is Himself the author of the instruments He employs for the communication of His messages to men and has framed them into precisely the instruments He desired for the exact communication of His message. There is just ground for the expectation that He will use all the instruments He employs according to their natures; intelligent beings therefore as intelligent beings, moral agents as moral agents. But there is no just ground for asserting that God is incapable of employing the intelligent beings He has Himself created and formed to His will, to proclaim His messages purely as He gives them to them; or of making truly the possession of rational minds conceptions which they have themselves had no part in creating. And there is no ground for imagining that God is unable to frame His own message in the language of the organs of His revelation without its thereby ceasing to be, because expressed in a fashion natural to these organs, therefore purely His message. One would suppose it to lie in the very nature of the case that if the Lord makes any revelation to men, He would do it in the language of men; or, to individualize more explicitly, in the language of the man He employs as the organ of His revelation; and that naturally means, not the language of his nation or circle merely, but his own particular language, inclusive of all that gives individuality to his self-expression. We may speak of this, if we will, as "the accommodation of the revealing God to the several prophetic individualities." But we should avoid thinking of it externally and therefore mechanically, as if the revealing Spirit artificially phrased the message which He gives through each prophet in the particular forms of speech proper to the individuality of each, so as to create the illusion that the message comes out of the heart of the prophet himself. Precisely what the prophets affirm is that their messages do not come out of their own hearts and do not represent the workings of their own spirits. Nor is there any illusion in the phenomenon we are contemplating; and it is a much more intimate, and, we may add, a much more interesting phenomenon than an external "accommodation" of speech to individual habitudes. It includes, on the one hand, the "accommodation" of the prophet, through his total preparation, to the speech in which the revelation to be given through him is to be clothed; and on the other involves little more than the consistent carrying into detail of the broad principle that God uses the instruments He employs in accordance with their natures.

No doubt, on adequate occasion, the very stones might cry out by the power of God, and dumb beasts speak, and mysterious voices sound forth from the void; and there have not been lacking instances in which men have been compelled by the same power to speak what they would not, and in languages whose very sounds were strange to their ears. But ordinarily when God the Lord would speak to men He avails Himself of the services of a human tongue with which to speak, and He employs this tongue according to its nature as a tongue and according to the particular nature of the tongue which He employs. It is vain to say that the message delivered through the instrumentality of this tongue is conditioned at least in its form by the tongue by which it is spoken, if not, indeed, limited, curtailed, in some degree determined even in its matter, by it. Not only was it God the Lord who made the tongue, and who made this particular tongue with all its peculiarities, not without regard to the message He would deliver through it; but His control of it is perfect and complete, and it is as absurd to say that He cannot speak His message by it purely without that message suffering change from the peculiarities of its tone and modes of enunciation, as it would be to say that no new truth can be announced in any language because the elements of speech by the combination of which the truth in question is announced are already in existence with their fixed range of connotation. The marks of the several individualities imprinted on the messages of the prophets, in other words, are only a part of the general fact that these messages are couched in human language, and in no way beyond that general fact affect their purity as direct communications from God.

6. Revelation by Inspiration:

A new set of problems is raised by the mode of revelation which we have called "concursive operation." This mode of revelation differs from prophecy, properly so called, precisely by the employment in it, as is not done in prophecy, of the total personality of the organ of revelation, as a factor. It has been common to speak of the mode of the Spirit's action in this form of revelation, therefore, as an assistance, a superintendence, a direction, a control, the meaning being that the effect aimed at-- the discovery and enunciation of divine truth--is attained through the action of the human powers--historical research, logical reasoning, ethical thought, religious aspiration--acting not by themselves, however, but under the prevailing assistance, superintendence, direction, control of the Divine Spirit. This manner of speaking has the advantage of setting this mode of revelation sharply in contrast with prophetic revelation, as involving merely a determining, and not, as in prophetic revelation, a supercessive action of the revealing Spirit. We are warned, however, against pressing this discrimination too far by the inclusion of the whole body of Scripture in such passages as 2Pe 1:20 f in the category of prophecy, and the assignment of their origin not to a mere "leading" but to the "bearing" of the Holy Spirit. In any event such terms as assistance, superintendence, direction, control, inadequately express the nature of the Spirit's action in revelation by "concursive operation." The Spirit is not to be conceived as standing outside of the human powers employed for the effect in view, ready to supplement any inadequacies they may show and to supply any defects they may manifest, but as working confluently in, with and by them, elevating them, directing them, controlling them, energizing them, so that, as His instruments, they rise above themselves and under His inspiration do His work and reach His aim. The product, therefore, which is attained by their means is His product through them. It is this fact which gives to the process the right to be called actively, and to the product the right to be called passively, a revelation. Although the circumstance that what is done is done by and through the action of human powers keeps the product in form and quality in a true sense human, yet the confluent operation of the Holy Spirit throughout the whole process raises the result above what could by any possibility be achieved by mere human powers and constitutes it expressly a supernatural product. The human traits are traceable throughout its whole extent, but at bottom it is a divine gift, and the language of Paul is the most proper mode of speech that could be applied to it: "Which things also we speak, not in words which man's wisdom teacheth, but which the Spirit teacheth" (1Co 2:13); "The things which I write unto you .... are the commandment of the Lord" (1Co 14:37).

7. Complete Revelation of God in Christ:

It is supposed that all the forms of special or redemptive revelation which underlie and give its content to the religion of the Bible may without violence be subsumed under one or another of these three modes--external manifestation, internal suggestion, and concursive operation. All, that is, except the culminating revelation, not through, but in, Jesus Christ. As in His person, in which dwells all the fullness of the Godhead bodily, He rises above all classification and is sui generis; so the revelation accumulated in Him stands outside all the divers portions and divers manners in which otherwise revelation has been given and sums up in itself all that has been or can be made known of God and of His redemption. He does not so much make a revelation of God as Himself is the revelation of God; He does not merely disclose God's purpose of redemption, He is unto us wisdom from God, and righteousness and sanctification and redemption. The theophanies are but faint shadows in comparison with His manifestation of God in the flesh. The prophets could prophesy only as the Spirit of Christ which was in them testified, revealing to them as to servants one or another of the secrets of the Lord

Yahweh; from Him as His Son, Yahweh has no secrets, but whatsoever the Father knows that the Son knows also. Whatever truth men have been made partakers of by the Spirit of truth is His (for all things whatsoever the Father hath are His) and is taken by the Spirit of truth and declared to men that He may be glorified. Nevertheless, though all revelation is thus summed up in Him, we should not fail to note very carefully that it would also be all sealed up in Him--so little is revelation conveyed by fact alone, without the word--had it not been thus taken by the Spirit of truth and declared unto men. The entirety of the New Testament is but the explanatory word accompanying and giving its effect to the fact of Christ. And when this fact was in all its meaning made the possession of men, revelation was completed and in that sense ceased. Jesus Christ is no less the end of revelation than He is the end of the law.

IV. Biblical Terminology.

1. The Ordinary Forms:

There is not much additional to be learned concerning the nature and processes of revelation, from the terms currently employed in Scripture to express the idea. These terms are ordinarily the common words for disclosing, making known, making manifest, applied with more or less heightened significance to supernatural acts or effects in kind. In the English Bible (the King James Version) the verb "reveal" occurs about 51 times, of which 22 are in the Old Testament and 29 in the New Testament. In the Old Testament the word is always the rendering of a Hebrew term galah, or its Aramaic equivalent gelah, the root meaning of which appears to be "nakedness." When applied to revelation, it seems to hint at the removal of obstacles to perception or the uncovering of objects to perception. In the New Testament the word "reveal" is always (with the single exception of Lu 2:35) the rendering of a Greek term apokalupto (but in 2Th 1:7; 1Pe 4:13 the corresponding noun apokalupsis), which has a very similar basal significance with its Hebrew parallel. As this Hebrew word formed no substantive in this sense, the noun "revelation" does not occur in the English Old Testament, the idea being expressed, however, by other Hebrew terms variously rendered. It occurs in the English New Testament, on the other hand, about a dozen times, and always

24

as the rendering of the substantive corresponding to the verb rendered "reveal" (apokalupsis). On the face of the English Bible, the terms "reveal," "revelation" bear therefore uniformly the general sense of "disclose," "disclosure." The idea is found in the Bible, however, much more frequently than the terms "reveal" "revelation" in English Versions of the Bible. Indeed, the Hebrew and Greek terms exclusively so rendered occur more frequently in this sense than in this rendering in the English Bible. And by their side there stand various other terms which express in one way or another the general conception.

In the New Testament the verb phaneroo, with the general sense of making manifest, manifesting, is the most common of these. It differs from apokalupto as the more general and external term from the more special and inward. Other terms also are occasionally used: epiphaneia, "manifestation" (2Th 2:8; 1Ti 6:14; 2Ti 1:10; 4:1; Tit 2:13; compare epiphaino, Tit 2:11; 3:4); deiknuo (Re 1:1; 17:1; 22:1, 6, 8; compare Ac 9:16; 1Ti 4:15); exegomai (Joh 1:18), of which, however, only one perhaps-- chrematizo (Matt 2:12, 22; Lu 2:20; Ac 10:22; Heb. 8:5; 11:7; 12:25); p chrematismos (Ro 11:4)--calls for particular notice as in a special way, according to its usage, expressing the idea of a divine communication.

In the Old Testament, the common Hebrew verb for "seeing" (ra'ah) is used in its appropriate stems, with God as the subject, for "appearing," "showing": "the Lord appeared unto .... "; "the word which the Lord showed me." And from this verb not only is an active substantive formed which supplied the more ancient designation of the official organ of revelation: ro'eh, "seer"; but also objective substantives, mar'ah, and mar'eh, which were used to designate the thing seen in a revelation--the "vision." By the side of these terms there were others in use, derived from a root which supplies to the Aramaic its common word for "seeing," but in Hebrew has a somewhat more pregnant meaning, chazah. Its active derivative, chozeh, was a designation of a prophet which remained in occasional use, alternating with the more customary nabhi', long after ro'eh, had become practically obsolete; and its passive derivatives chazon, chizzayon, chazuth, machazeh provided the ordinary terms for the substance of the revelation or "vision." The distinction between the two sets of terms, derived respectively from ra'ah and chazah, while not to be unduly pressed, seems to lie in the direction that the former suggests external manifestations and the latter internal revelations. The ro'eh is he to whom divine manifestations, the chozeh he to whom divine communications, have been vouchsafed; the mar'eh is an appearance, the chazon and its companions a vision. It may be of interest to observe that mar'ah is the term employed in Nu 12:6, while it is chazon which commonly occurs in the headings of the written prophecies to indicate their revelatory character. From this it may possibly be inferred that in the former passage it is the mode, in the latter the contents of the revelation that is emphasized. Perhaps a like distinction may be traced between the chazon of Da 8:15 and the mar'eh of the next verse. The ordinary verb for "knowing," yadha`, expressing in its causative stems the idea of making known, informing, is also very naturally employed, with God as its subject, in the sense of revealing, and that, in accordance with the natural sense of the word, with a tendency to pregnancy of implication, of revealing effectively, of not merely uncovering to observation, but making to know. Accordingly, it is paralleled riot merely with galah (Ps 98:2: `The Lord hath made known his salvation; his righteousness hath he displayed in the sight of the nation'), but also with such terms as lamadh (Ps 25:4: `Make known to me thy ways, O Lord: teach me thy paths'). This verb yadha` forms no substantive in the sense of "revelation" (compare da`ath, Nu 24:16; Ps 19:3).

2. "Word of Yahweh" and "Torah":

The most common vehicles of the idea of "revelation" in the Old Testament are, however, two expressions which are yet to be mentioned. These are the phrase, "word of Yahweh," and the term commonly but inadequately rendered in the English Versions of the Bible by "law." The former (debhar Yahweh, varied to debhar 'Elohim or debhar ha-'Elohim; compare ne'um Yahweh, massa' Yahweh) occurs scores of times and is at once the simplest and the most colorless designation of a divine communication. By the latter (torah), the proper meaning of which is "instruction," a strong implication of authoritativeness is conveyed; and, in this sense, it becomes what may be called the technical designation of a specifically divine communication. The two are not infrequently brought together, as in Isa 1:10: "Hear the word of Yahweh, ye rulers of Sodom; give ear unto the law (margin "teaching") of our God, ye people of Gomorrah"; or Isa 2:3 margin; Mic 4:2: "For out of Zion shall go forth the law (margin "instruction"), and the word of Yahweh from Jerusalem." Both terms are used for any divine communication of whatever extent; and both came to be employed to express the entire body of divine revelation, conceived as a unitary whole. In this comprehensive usage, the emphasis of the one came to fall more on the graciousness, and of the other more on the authoritativeness of this body of divine revelation; and both passed into the New Testament with these implications. "The word of God," or simply "the word," comes thus to mean in the New Testament just the gospel, "the word of the proclamation of redemption, that is, all that which God has to say to man, and causes to be said" looking to his salvation. It expresses, in a word, precisely what we technically speak of as God's redemptive revelation. "The law," on the other hand, means in this New Testament use, just the whole body of the authoritative instruction which God has given men. It expresses, in other words, what we commonly speak of as God's supernatural revelation. The two things, of course, are the same: God's authoritative revelation is His gracious revelation; God's redemptive revelation is His supernatural revelation. The two terms merely look at the one aggregate of revelation from two aspects, and each emphasizes its own aspect of this one aggregated revelation.

Now, this aggregated revelation lay before the men of the New Testament in a written form, and it was impossible to speak freely of it without consciousness of and at least occasional reference to its written form. Accordingly we hear of a Word of God that is written, (Joh 15:25; 1Co 15:54), and the Divine Word is naturally contrasted with mere tradition, as if its written form were of its very idea (Mr 7:10); indeed, the written body of revelation--with an emphasis on its written form--is designated expressly `the prophetic word' (2Pe 1:19).

3. "The Scriptures":

More distinctly still, "the Law" comes to be thought of as a written, not exactly, code, but body of Divinely authoritative instructions. The phrase, "It is written in your law" (Joh 10:34; 15:25; Ro 3:19; 1Co 14:21), acquires the precise sense of, "It is set forth in your authoritative Scriptures, all the content of which is `law,' that is, divine instruction." Thus, "the Word of

27

God," "the Law," came to mean just the written body of revelation, what we call, and what the New Testament writers called, in the same high sense which we give the term, "the Scriptures." These "Scriptures" are thus identified with the revelation of God, conceived as a well-defined corpus, and two conceptions rise before us which have had a determining part to play in the history of Christianity--the conception of an authoritative Canon of Scripture, and the conception of this Canon of Scripture as just the Word of God written. The former conception was thrown into prominence in opposition to the Gnostic heresies in the earliest age of the church, and gave rise to a richly varied mode of speech concerning the Scriptures, emphasizing their authority in legal language, which goes back to and rests on the Biblical. usage of "Law." The latter it was left to the Reformation to do justice to in its struggle against, on the one side, the Romish depression of the Scriptures in favor of the traditions of the church, and on the other side the Enthusiasts' supercession of them in the interests of the "inner Word." When Tertullian, on the one hand, speaks of the Scriptures as an "Instrument," a legal document, his terminology has an express warrant in the Scriptures' own usage of torah, "law," to designate their entire content. And when John Gerhard argues that "between the Word of God and Sacred Scripture, taken in a material sense, there is no real difference," he is only declaring plainly what is definitely implied in the New Testament use of "the Word of God" with the written revelation in mind. What is important to recognize is that the Scriptures themselves represent the Scriptures as not merely containing here and there the record of revelations--"words of God," toroth--given by God, but as themselves, in all their extent, a revelation, an authoritative body of gracious instructions from God; or, since they alone, of all the revelations which God may have given, are extant--rather as the Revelation, the only "Word of God" accessible to men, in all their parts "law," that is, authoritative instruction from God.

Review Questions

- What is the difference between general and special revelation?
- Why was revelation different in the Garden of Eden?

- How does God reveal himself to those who have yet to hear the Gospel?

- What is the process of revelation?

- What is the place of revelation among the redemptive acts of God?

- What are the modes of revelation?

- What is the primary meaning of the Hebrew and Greek words for prophet?

- How are we to understand revelation by inspiration?

CHAPTER 2 Inspiration and Inerrancy in the Writing Process

In recent years, a number of scholars have suggested that Jesus could not read, and that in all likelihood none of his disciples could read either. They maintain this because of studies that have concluded that rates of literacy in the Roman Empire were quite low, and that Jesus and his earliest followers were probably not exceptions.[1]

Literacy in the First Century

How can we, modern readers, know so much about letters from the ancient Roman Empire? We have two different sources that provide us some insight into the writer and his letters. Lucius or Marcus Annaeus Seneca, known as **Seneca the Elder** (54 B.C.E.-39 C.E.), was a Roman rhetorician and writer, born of a wealthy equestrian family of Cordoba, Hispania. Seneca lived through the reigns of three significant emperors: Augustus, Tiberius, and Caligula. For our purpose here we are particularly interested in his letters, which were published; i.e. someone paid to have a scribe produce a copy of them. As was the case with many works of antiquity, the process was repeated over and over again throughout the centuries. Today, we have critical editions of them.

Our other source for insight into the development of the letter writing process is found in the letters of ordinary people, uncovered by archaeologists. These were never published, as they were simply discarded after they served their purpose. In many cases, in order to save costs, these writers would simply flip a letter over and use the other side for something else. Many such letters ended up in garbage dumps. However, some recipients of these letters valued them, so they stored them like some treasure.

---

[1] Craig A. Evans (2012-03-16). *Jesus and His World: The Archaeological Evidence* (Kindle Locations 1403-1406). Westminster John Knox Press. Kindle Edition.

Therefore, when archaeologists uncovered homes, these letters would be found within the ruins of the home. In some cases, they were even buried with the deceased because they were so valued. Hundreds of thousands of letters have been discovered over the past century by archaeologists. These were the work of common folk, writing about everyday things.

Most of us have heard of Marcus Tullius Cicero, or simply Cicero (106 B.C.E.–43 B.C.E.), who was a Roman philosopher, politician, lawyer, orator, political theorist, consul, and constitutionalist. He came from a wealthy municipal family in Rome. In his everyday affairs, he penned letters in order to correspond with others. However, while Cicero was writing letters to one person, he knew that others would be reading them as well. Therefore, he took advantage of these opportunities to use writing to communicate points persuasively, using logic and reason, philosophical arguments, and the like. His letters grew from very short letters to far longer, intricate rhetorical letters.

We find yet another famous Roman named Seneca in the days of the apostle Paul. He was the second son of Seneca the Elder. Lucius Annaeus Seneca, or simply **Seneca the Younger** (c. 4 B.C.E.–65 C.E.), was a Roman Stoic philosopher, statesman, and dramatist, i.e., a very famous, skilled, and effective speaker. As for written works, Seneca is known for twelve philosophical essays, 124 letters to Lucilius Junior, nine tragedies, and a satire, which is uncertain. Seneca was a representative of the Silver Age of Latin literature. In his letters to his friend Lucilius, dealing with moral issues, he delved into philosophical ideas, setting aside the simple and bare letters of the day for something far more complex.

The apostle Paul, as we have seen, used personal letters and letter carriers as a substitute until he could visit churches and key people. He produced through his scribe Tertius 433 verses, 7,111 words in the book of Romans, which would have taken two days to copy. Like the skilled rhetoricians before him, Paul knew that many others would be reading his letters. In fact, he exhorted them to do so. – Colossians 4:16.

We should note that the level of literacy in the first century is a somewhat subjective measurement, because of the limited evidence that is available, as well as one's interpretation of that evidence. Consider as an analogy the historian today, as compared to the historian during the first few centuries of Christianity. Today, we are capable of covering almost anything that goes on in life, from the most insignificant to the most noteworthy. We in the United States may watch live on television or a laptop as some firefighters in New Zealand rescue a puppy that had been trapped in a storm drain. Then again, we can observe a 9.0 earthquake as it hits Japan, causing the deaths of over 15,000 people.

What about the first few centuries of Jesus, the apostles, and the earliest Christians? The coverage of people, places, and events are not even remotely comparable. The coverage at that time was of the most prominent people, like Seneca the Elder, Cicero, Seneca the Younger, Mark Antony, and Augustus, i.e., the emperor of Rome, senators, generals, the wealthy, with very little press being given to the lower officials, let alone the lower class. We do not have much information on Pontius Pilate at all, but what we do have is an exception to the rule.

History from antiquity, then, is recoverable but incomplete due to the limited extent and frequently tendentious nature of the sources. Ancient historiography, more than its modern counterpart, is to a greater degree approximate or provisional. A new discovery may alter previous perceptions. Until the discovery of Claudius's Letter to the Alexandrians, written on his accession in 41 but lost until modern times, that emperor's steely resolve could not have been guessed. In short, evidence from Greco-Roman antiquity is fragmentary, generally devoted to "important" people and events and its texts overtly "interpreted." (Barnett 2005, 13)

Literacy in the first century was determined by being able to read, not write.[2] The need for writing today is far greater than antiquity. Richards offers an excellent analogy when he says, "I am right handed, so to pen a long paper with my left hand would be quite difficult, and not very legible. The man of

---

[2] (Richards, Paul And First-Century Letter Writing: Secretaries, Composition and Collection 2004, 28)

antiquity would write with the same difficulty because the need to write was so seldom."[3] This author finds this to be true of himself, now that we have entered an era of texting and typing. I have not written a paper by hand in years. When I fill out a form or even sign my name, I struggle to write, because it is so seldom required. Many have argued that the lower class of antiquity was almost entirely illiterate. However, recent research shows that this was not the case,[4] as literacy was more of an everyday need than they had thought.[5] However, let us assume for the sake of discussion that literacy was very low among the lower class, and even relatively low among the upper class, who had the ability to pay for the service.

What does this say about individual Christians throughout the Roman Empire? It is believed that more than 30–40 million people lived in the combined eastern and western Roman Empire (50–200 C.E.). Now, assume that statistically, the literacy rate is low in a certain area, or in a certain city, like Rome (slave population). Does this mean that everyone is illiterate in that region or city? Do we equate the two? If we accept the belief that the lower class were likely to be illiterate, meaning they could not write, or struggled to write; what does this really mean for Christianity? Very little, because if there are 40-100 million people living throughout the Roman Empire and one million of them were Christian by 125-150 C.E., we are only referring to one or two percent of the population. There is no way to arrive at an exact statistical level of literacy for this tiny selection, in a time period when history focused on the prominent. If a person from that period said anything about the lower class, this was only

---

[3] (Richards, Paul And First-Century Letter Writing: Secretaries, Composition and Collection 2004, 28)

[4] "Throughout the Hellenistic and Roman world the distinction prevailed in that there were educated people who were proficient readers and writers, less educated ones who could read but hardly write, some who were readers alone, some of them only able to read slowly or with difficulty and some who were illiterate."--Millard, Alan Reading and Writing in the Time of Jesus (Sheffield, Sheffield Academic Press, 2000), p. 154

[5] Exler, Form. P. 126 warns, "The papyri discovered in Egypt have shown that the art of writing was more widely, and more popularly, known in the past, than some scholars have been inclined to think." For example, see PZen. 6, 66, POxy. 113,294, 394, 528, 530, 531 and especially 3057.

based on the sphere of whom he knew or what he had seen in his life, which would be very limited when compared to the whole. The last 20 years or so has seen many new directions in the field of literacy in the ancient world. Johnson and Parker offer the following.

> The moment seems right, therefore, to try to formulate more interesting, productive ways of talking about the conception and construction of 'literacies' in the ancient world—literacy not in the sense of whether 10 percent or 30 percent of people in the ancient world could read or write, but in the sense of text-oriented events embedded in particular sociocultural contexts. The volume in your hands [ANCIENT LITERACIES] was constructed as a forum in which selected leading scholars were challenged to rethink from the ground up how students of classical antiquity might best approach the question of literacy, and how that investigation might materially intersect with changes in the way that literacy is now viewed in other disciplines. The result is intentionally pluralistic: theoretical reflections, practical demonstrations, and combinations of the two share equal space in the effort to chart a new course. Readers will come away, with food for thought of many types: new ways of thinking about specific elements of literacy in antiquity, such as the nature of personal libraries, or the place and function of bookshops in antiquity; new constructivist questions, such as what constitutes reading communities and how they fashion themselves; new takes on the public sphere, such how literacy intersects with commercialism, or with the use of public spaces, or with the construction of civic identity; new essentialist questions, such as what "book" and "reading" signify in antiquity, why literate cultures develop, or why literate cultures matter. (Johnson and Parker 2011, 3-4)

Literacy and Early Jewish Education

During the first seven years of Christianity (29-36 C.E.), three and a half with Jesus' ministry and three and a half after his ascension, only Jewish people became disciples of Christ and formed the newly founded Christian congregation. In 36 C.E. the first gentile was baptized: Cornelius.[6] From that time forward Gentiles came into the Christian congregations. However, the church still consisted largely of Jewish converts. What do we know of the Jewish family, as far as education? Within the nation of Israel, everyone was strongly encouraged to be literate. The texts of Deuteronomy 6:8-9 and 11:20 were figurative (not to be taken literally). However, we are to ascertain what was meant by the figurative language, and that meaning is what we take literally.

Deuteronomy 6:8-9 English Standard Version (ESV)

[8] You shall bind them [God's Word] as a sign on your hand, and they shall be as frontlets between your eyes. [9] You shall write them on the doorposts of your house and on your gates.

Deuteronomy 11:20 English Standard Version (ESV)

[20] You shall write them on the doorposts of your house and on your gates,

The command to bind God's Word "as a sign on your hand," denoted constant remembrance and attention. The command that the Word of God was "to be as frontlet bands between your eyes," denoted that the Law should be kept before their eyes constantly, so that wherever they looked, whatever was before them, they would see the law before them. Therefore, while figurative, these texts implied that Jewish children grew up being taught how to read and to write. The Gezer Calendar (ancient Hebrew writing), dated to the 10th-century B.C.E., is believed by some scholars to be a schoolboy's memory exercise.

Philo of Alexandria (20 B.C.E.–50 C. E.) a Hellenistic Jewish philosopher, whose first language was Greek, had this to say about Jewish parents and how they taught their Children the Law and how to read it. Philo stated, "All men guard their own customs, but this is especially true of the Jewish nation. Holding that the laws are oracles vouchsafed by God and having been trained [paideuthentes] in this doctrine from their earliest years,

---

[6] Cornelius was a centurion, an army officer in charge of a unit of foot soldiers, i.e., in command of 100 soldiers of the Italian band.

they carry the likenesses of the commandments enshrined in their souls." (Borgen 1997, 187) This certainly involved the ability to read and write at a competent level. Josephus (37-100 C.E.), the first-century Jewish historian, writes, "Our principle care of all is this, to educate our children [*paidotrophian*] well; and we think it to be the most necessary business of our whole life to observe the laws that have been given us, and to keep those rules of piety that have been delivered down to us." (Whiston 1987, Against Apion 1.60) Even allowing for an overemphasis for apologetic purposes; clearly, Jesus was carefully grounded in the Word of God (Hebrew Old Testament), as was true of other Jews of the time. Josephus also says,

"but for our people, if anybody do but ask any one of them about our laws, he will more readily tell them all than he will tell his own name, and this in consequence of our having learned them immediately as soon as ever we became sensible of anything, and of our having them, as it were engraven on our souls. Our transgressors of them are but few; and it is impossible when any do offend, to escape punishment." (Whiston 1987, Against Apion 2.178) He also says: "[the Law] also commands us to bring those children up in learning [*grammata* paideuein] and to exercise them in the laws, and make them acquainted with the acts of their predecessors, in order to their imitation of them, and that they may be nourished up in the laws from their infancy, and might neither transgress them, nor yet have any pretense for their ignorance of them." (Whiston 1987, Against Apion 2.204) Again, this clearly involves at a minimum the ability to read and write at a competent level.

From the above, we find that the Jewish family education revolved around the study of the Mosaic Law. If their children were going to live by the Law, they needed to know what it says, as well as understand it. If they were going to know and understand the Law, this would require the ability to read it, and hopefully apply it. Emil Schurer writes: "All zeal for education in the family, the school and the synagogue aimed at making *the whole people a people of the law*. The common man too was to know what the law commanded, and not only to know but to do it. His whole life was to be ruled according to the norm of the law; obedience thereto was to become a fixed custom, and departure therefrom an inward impossibility. On the whole, this object was to a great degree attained." (Schurer 1890, Vol. 4, p. 89) Scott writes that "from at least the time of Ezra's reading of the law (Neh. 8), education was a public process; study of the law was the focus of Jewish society as a whole. It was a lifelong commitment to all men. It began with the very young. The Mishnah[7] requires that children be taught 'therein one year or two years before [they are of age], that they may become versed in the commandments.' Other sources set different ages for beginning formal studies, some as early as five years."[8] (Scott 1995, 257)

It may be that both Philo and Josephus are presenting their readers with an idyllic picture, and what they have to say could possibly refer primarily to wealthy Jewish families who could afford formal education. However, this would be shortsighted, for the Israelites had long been a people who valued the ability to read and write competently. In the apocryphal account of 4 Maccabees 18:10-19, a mother addresses her seven sons, who would be martyred, reminding them of their father's teaching. There is nothing in the account to suggest that they were from a wealthy family. Herein the mother referred to numerous historical characters throughout the Old Testament and quoted from numerous books – Isaiah 43.2; Psalm 34:19; Proverbs 3:18; Ezekiel 37:3; Deuteronomy 32:39.

Jesus would have received his education from three sources. As was made clear from the above, Joseph, Jesus' stepfather would have played a major role in his education. Paul said that young Timothy was trained in "the sacred writings" by his mother, Eunice, and his grandmother Lois. (2 Tim. 1:5; 3:15) Certainly, if Timothy received education in the law from his mother because his Father was a Greek (Acts 16:1), no doubt Jesus did as well after Joseph died.

Jesus would have also received education in the Scriptures from the attendant at the synagogue. In the first-century C.E., the synagogue was a place of instruction, not a place of sacrifices. The people carried out their sacrifices to God at the temple. The

---

[7] The Mishnah was the primary body of Jewish civil and religious law, forming the first part of the Talmud.

[8] Mishnah Yoma 8:4

exercises within the synagogue covered such areas as praise, prayer, and recitation and reading of the Scriptures, in addition to expository preaching. – Mark 12:40; Luke 20:47

> Before any instruction in the holy laws and unwritten customs are taught... from their swaddling clothes by parents and teachers and educators to believe in God, the one Father, and Creator of the world. (Philo *Legatio ad Gaium* 115.)

The Mishnah tells us the age that this formal instruction would have begun, "At five years old one is fit for the scripture... at thirteen for the commandments." (Mishnah *Abot* 5.21.) Luke 4:20 tells of the time Jesus stood to read from the scroll of Isaiah in the synagogue in Nazareth, and once finished, "he rolled up the scroll and gave it back to the attendant." An attendant such as this one would have educated Jesus, starting at the age of five. As Jesus grew up in Nazareth, he "increased in wisdom and in stature and in favor with God and man." (Lu 2:52) Jesus and his half-brothers and sisters would have been known to the people of the city of Nazareth, which was nothing more than a village in Jesus' day. "As was his custom, [Jesus] went to the synagogue on the Sabbath day," each week. (Matt. 13:55, 56; Lu. 4:16) While Jesus would have been an exceptional student, unlike anything that the Nazareth synagogue would have ever seen, we must keep in mind that the disciples would have been going through similar experiences as they grew up in Galilee. Great emphasis was laid on the need for every Jew to have an accurate knowledge of the Law. Josephus wrote,

> for he [God] did not suffer the guilt of ignorance to go on without punishment, but demonstrated the law to be the best and the most necessary instruction of all others, permitting the people to leave off their other employments, and to assemble together for the hearing of the law, and learning it exactly, and this not once or twice, or oftener, but every week; which thing all the other legislators seem to have neglected. (Whiston 1987, Against Apion 2.175)

The high priest questioned Jesus about his disciples and his teaching. Jesus answered him, "I have spoken openly to the world. I have always taught in synagogues and in the temple,

where all Jews come together. I have said nothing in secret."
(John 18:19-20) We know that another source of knowledge and
wisdom of Jesus came from the Father. Jesus said, "My teaching is
not mine, but his who sent me," i.e., the Father. – John 7:16.

Mark 1:22 English Standard Version (ESV)	Mark 1:27 English Standard Version (ESV)
[22] And they were **astonished at his teaching**, for he taught them as **one who had authority**, and not as the scribes.	[27] And they were all **amazed**, so that they questioned among themselves, saying, "What is this? A new teaching **with authority**!

At first, in the days of Ezra and Nehemiah, the priests served
as scribes. (Ezra 7:1-6) The scribes referred to here in the Gospel
of Mark are more than copyists of Scripture. They were
professionally trained scholars, who were experts in the Mosaic
Law. As was said above, a great emphasis was laid on the need
for every Jew to have an accurate knowledge of the Law.
Therefore, those who gave a great deal of their life and time to
acquiring an immense amount of knowledge were admired,
becoming scholars, forming a group separate from the priests,
creating a systematic study of the law, as well as its exposition,
which became a professional occupation. By the time of Jesus,
these scribes were experts in more than the Mosaic Law (entire
Old Testament actually) as they became experts on the previous
experts from centuries past, quoting them in addition to quoting
Scripture. In other words, if there was any Scriptural decision to
be made, these scribes quoted previous experts in the law, i.e.,
their comments on the law, as opposed to quoting applicable
Scripture itself. The scribes were among the "teachers of the law,"
also referred to as "lawyers." (Lu 5:17; 11:45) The people were
astonished and **amazed** at Jesus' **teaching** and **authority**
because he did not quote previous teachers of the law, but rather
referred to Scripture alone as his authority, along with his
exposition.

Jesus' Childhood Visits to Jerusalem

Only one event from Jesus' childhood is given to us, and it is found in the Gospel of Luke. We have addressed it earlier, so what lies below can serve as a refresher. It certainly adds heavy circumstantial evidence to the fact that Jesus could read and was literate.

Luke 2:41-47 Updated American standard Version (UASV)

⁴¹ Now His parents went to Jerusalem every year at the Feast of the Passover. ⁴² And <u>when he [Jesus] was twelve years old</u>, they went up according to the custom of the feast. ⁴³ And after the days were completed, while they were returning, the boy Jesus stayed behind in Jerusalem. And his parents did not know it, ⁴⁴ but supposing him to be in the company, they went a day's journey; and they began looking for him among their relatives and acquaintances. ⁴⁵ and when they did not find him, they returned to Jerusalem, looking for him. ⁴⁶ Then, it occurred, after three days they <u>found him in the temple</u>, sitting in the midst of the teachers and **listening** to them and **questioning them**. ⁴⁷ And all those listening to him were **amazed at his understanding** and his answers.

As we pointed out earlier in chapter 2, this was no 12-year-old boy's questions of curiosity. The Greek indicates that Jesus, at the age of twelve did not ask childlike questions, looking for answers, but was likely challenging the thinking of these Jewish religious leaders.

This incident is far more magnificent than one might first realize. Kittel's *Theological Dictionary of the New Testament* helps the reader to appreciate that the Greek word *eperotao* (to ask, to question, to demand of), for "questioning" was far more than the Greek word erotao (to ask, to request, to entreat), for a boy's inquisitiveness. *Eperotao* can refer to questioning, which one might hear in a judicial hearing, such as a scrutiny, inquiry, counter questioning, even the "probing and cunning questions of the Pharisees and Sadducees," for instance those we find at Mark 10:2 and 12:18-23.

The same dictionary continues: "In [the] face of this usage it may be asked whether . . . [Luke] 2:46 denotes, not so much the questioning curiosity of the boy, but rather His successful disputing. [Verse] 47 would fit in well with the latter view." Rotherham's translation of verse 47 presents it as a dramatic confrontation: "Now all who heard him were beside themselves, because of his understanding and his answers." Robertson's Word Pictures in the New Testament says that their constant amazement means, "they stood out of themselves as if their eyes were bulging out."

After returning to Jerusalem, and three days of searching, Joseph and Mary found young Jesus in the temple, questioning the Jewish religious leaders, at which "they were astounded." (Luke 2:48) Robertson said of this, "second aorist passive indicative of an old Greek word [*ekplesso*]), to strike out, drive out by a blow. Joseph and Mary 'were struck out' by what they saw and heard. Even they had not fully realized the power in this wonderful boy."[9] Thus, at twelve years old, Jesus, only a boy, is already evidencing that he is a great teacher and defender of truth. BDAG says, "to cause to be filled with amazement to the point of being overwhelmed, amaze, astound, overwhelm (literally, Strike out of one's senses).[10]

Some 18 years later Jesus again confronted the Pharisees with these types of interrogative questions, so much so that not "anyone [of them] dare from that day on to ask him any more questions." (Matthew 22:41-46) The Sadducees fared no better when Jesus responded to them on the subject of the resurrection: "And no one dared to ask him any more questions." (Luke 20:27-40) The scribes were silenced just the same after they got into an exchange with Jesus: "And from then on no one dared ask him any more questions." (Mark 12:28-34) Clearly, this insight into Jesus' life and ministry provide us with evidence that he had the ability to read very well and likely write. There is the fact that Jesus was also divine. However, he was also fully human, and he grew, progressing in wisdom, because of his studies in the Scriptures.

---

[9] A.T. Robertson, Word Pictures in the New Testament (Nashville, TN: Broadman Press, 1933), Lk 2:48.

[10] William Arndt, Frederick W. Danker and Walter Bauer, A Greek-English Lexicon of the New Testament and Other Early Christian Literature, 3rd ed. (Chicago: University of Chicago Press, 2000), 308.

Luke 2:40, 51-52 New American Standard Bible (NASB)

⁴⁰ The Child continued to grow and become strong, **increasing in wisdom**; and the grace of God was upon Him.

⁵¹ And He went down with them and came to Nazareth, and He continued in subjection to them; and His mother treasured all *these* things in her heart.

⁵² And Jesus **kept increasing in wisdom** and stature, and in favor with God and men.

Jesus was often called "Rabbi," which was used in a real or genuine *sense* as "teacher." (Mark 9:5; 11:21; 14:45; John 1:38, 49 etc.) We find *"Rabbo(u)ni"* (Mark 10:51; John 20:16) as well as its Greek equivalents, "schoolmaster" or "instructor" (*epistata*; Luke 5:5; 8:24, 45; 9:33, 49; 17:13) or "teacher" (*didaskalos*; Matt. 8:19; 9:11; 12:38; Mark 4:38; 5:35; 9:17; 10:17, 20; 12:14, 19, 32; Luke 19:39; John 1:38; 3:2). Jesus used these same terms for himself, as did his disciples, even his adversaries, and those with no affiliation.

Another inference that Jesus was literate comes from his constant reference to reading Scripture, when confronted by the Jewish religious leaders: law students, Pharisees, Scribes and the Sadducees. Jesus said, **"Have you not read** what David did when he was hungry, and those who were with him ... Or **have you not read in the Law** how on the Sabbath the priests in the temple profane the Sabbath and are guiltless? (Matt. 12:3, 5; reference to 1 Sam 21:6 and Num 28:9) Again, Jesus responded, **"Have you not read** that he who created them from the beginning made them male and female." (Matt. 19:3; paraphrase of Gen 1:27) Jesus said to them, "Yes; **have you never read**, "'Out of the mouth of infants and nursing babies you have prepared praise'?" (Matt. 21:16; quoting Psa. 8:2) Jesus said to them, **"Have you never read in the Scriptures**: "'The stone that the builders rejected has become the cornerstone; this was the Lord's doing, and it is marvelous in our eyes'? (Matt. 21:42; Reference to Isaiah 28:16) Jesus said to him, **"What is written in the Law? How do you read it?**" (Lu. 10:26) Many of these references or Scripture quotations were asked in such a way to his opponents; there is little doubt Jesus himself had read them.

When Jesus asked in an interrogative way, "have you not read," it was taken for granted that he had read them. Jesus referred to or quoted over 120 Scriptures in the dialogue that we have in the Gospels.

The data that have been surveyed are more easily explained in reference to a literate Jesus, a Jesus who could read the Hebrew Scriptures, could paraphrase and interpret them in Aramaic and could do so in a manner that indicated his familiarity with current interpretive tendencies in both popular circles (as in the synagogues) and in professional, even elite circles (as seen in debates with scribes, ruling priests and elders). Of course, to conclude that Jesus was literate is not necessarily to conclude that Jesus had received formal scribal training. The data do not suggest this. Jesus' innovative, experiential approach to Scripture and to Jewish faith seems to suggest the contrary.[11]

How did Jesus gain such wisdom? Jesus, although divine, was not born with this exceptional wisdom that he demonstrated at the age of twelve and kept increasing. It was acquired. (Deut. 17:18-19) This extraordinary wisdom was no exception to the norm, not even for the Son of God himself. (Luke 2:52) Jesus' knowledge was acquired by his studying the Hebrew Old Testament, enabling him to challenge the thinking of the Jewish religious leaders with his questions at the age of twelve. Therefore, Jesus had to be very familiar with the Hebrew Old Testament, as well the skill of reasoning from the Scriptures.

Were the Apostle Peter and John Uneducated?

Acts 4:13 English Standard Version (ESV)	Acts 4:13 New American Standard Bible (NASB)
[13] Now when they saw the boldness of Peter and John, and perceived that **they were**	[13] Now as they observed the confidence of Peter and John and understood that **they**

---

[11] (Evans, Jesus and His World: The Archaeological Evidence 2012)

uneducated, common men, they were astonished. And they recognized that they had been with Jesus.	were **uneducated** and **untrained men**, they were amazed, and *began* to recognize them as having been with Jesus.

How are we to understand the statement that Peter and John **were uneducated?** (ESV, NASB, HCSB, LEB and others) [*unlettered* (YLT) or *unlearned* (ASV)] This did not necessarily mean that they could not read and write, as the letters that were penned by these apostles (or their secretaries) testify that they could. What this means is that they were not educated in higher learning of the Hebrew schools, such as studying under someone like Gamaliel, as was the case with Paul (Ac 5:34-39; 22:3).[12] The Greek words literally read καταλαβομενοι [having perceived] οτι [that] ανθρωποι [men] αγραμματοι [unlettered] εισιν [they are] και [and] ιδιωται [untrained]. This means that the disciples were not educated in the rabbinic schools. It did not mean that they were illiterate. In other words, they lacked scribal training. In addition, ιδιωται [untrained], simply means that in comparison to professionally trained scribes of their day, they were not specialists, i.e., were not trained or expert in the scribal duties. This hardly constitutes the idea that they were illiterate.

It was the same reason that the Jewish religious leaders were surprised by the extensive knowledge that Jesus had. They said of him, "How is it that this man has learning when he has never studied?" (John 7:15) This is our best Scriptural evidence that Jesus could read. Let us break it down to what the religious leaders were really saying of Jesus. They asked πως [how] ουτος [this one] γραμματα [letters/writings] οιδεν [has known] μη [not] μεμαθηκως [have learned]. First, this is a reference to the fact that Jesus did not study at the Hebrew schools, i.e., scribal training. In other words, 'how does this one [Jesus] have knowledge of letters/writings, when he has not studied at the Hebrew schools. This question means more than Jesus' ability to

---

[12] Gamaliel was a Pharisee and a leading authority in the Sanhedrin, as well as a teacher of the law, of which Acts says, Paul was "educated at the feet of Gamaliel according to the strict manner of the law of our fathers." (Ac 22:3)

read because as we saw in the above, Jewish children were taught to read.

Another example: Luke 4:16-30 says that Jesus "came to Nazareth, where he had been brought up. And as was his custom, he went to the synagogue on the Sabbath day, and he stood up to read. And the scroll of the prophet Isaiah was given to him. He unrolled the scroll and found" (Lu 4:16-17) Jesus was able to take the scroll of Isaiah and read what is now known as Isaiah 61:1-2. While the parallel account in Mark 6:1-6 does not refer to Jesus reading this text, scholars have long known that the gospel writers shared the events through their separate viewpoints, i.e., they drew attention to what stood out to them, and what served their purpose for writing their Gospel accounts.

Within the Roman empire from the first to the fourth century, we find public writings in and throughout all of the cities. It encompasses inscriptions, which are "dedications, lists of names, imperial decrees, statements or reminders of law, quotations of famous men and even rather pedestrian things, such as directions. Many gravestones and tombs are inscribed with more than the name of the deceased; some have lengthy, even poetic obituaries; others have threats and curses against grave robbers (literate ones, evidently!). The impression one gains is that everybody was expected to be able to read; otherwise, what was the point of all of these expensive inscriptions, incised on stone?"[13] This impression does not end with inscriptions, because archaeology can extrapolate that between the fourth and sixth centuries C.E., millions upon millions of documents came out of Oxyrhynchus, just one city, based on the more than 1.5 million documents found in their garbage dumps. Of these, five hundred thousand have been recovered.

The **Library of Celsus** (45-ca. 120 C.E.) is an ancient Roman building in Ephesus (completed in 135 C.E.) which contained some 12,000 scrolls. The library was also built as a monumental tomb for Celsus. He is buried in a stone coffin beneath the library. The **Ancient Library of Alexandria**, Egypt (third-century to 30 B.C.E.), was one of the largest and most significant libraries of the ancient world. Most of the books were kept as papyrus scrolls.

---

[13] (Evans, Jesus and His World: The Archaeological Evidence 2012)

King Ptolemy II Philadelphus (309–246 B.C.E.) is believed to have set 500,000 scrolls as a goal for the library. Apparently, by the first century C.E., the library contained one million scrolls. The **Library of Pergamum** (Asia Minor) was one of the most significant libraries in the ancient world. It is said to have housed roughly 200,000 volumes. Historical records say that the library had a large main reading room. We have not even mentioned Rome, Athens, Corinth, Antioch (Syria), and the rest. The Mediterranean world from Alexander the Great (356-323 B.C.E.) to Constantine the Great (272-337 C.E.), some 700 years, saw hundreds of major libraries, as well as thousands of moderate to minor ones, with hundreds of millions of documents being written and read. Certainly, this does not suggest illiteracy, but literacy.

Some point out that "Celsus,[14] the first writer against Christianity, makes it a matter of mockery, that labourers, shoemakers, farmers, the most uninformed and clownish of men, should be zealous preachers of the Gospel."[15] Paul explained it this way: "For consider your calling, brothers: not many of you were wise according to worldly standards, not many were powerful, not many were of noble birth. But God chose what is foolish in the world to shame the wise; God chose what is weak in the world to shame the strong." (1 Cor. 1:26-27) It seems that these so-called illiterate Christians were able to grow from 120 in Jerusalem about 33 C.E., to some one million by 100 C.E., a mere 67 years later. This growth in the Christian population all came about because they effectively evangelized, using the Septuagint (Greek Old Testament). They were so effective with the Septuagint that the Jews abandoned it and went back to the Hebrew Old Testament.

In any case, Celsus was an enemy of Christianity. In addition, as was stated above, what Celsus observed was only within the sphere of his personal experiences. How many Christians could he

---

[14] This Celsus was a second-century Greek philosopher and opponent of early Christianity, who should not be confused with the previously mentioned Celsus, Roman Senator Tiberius Julius Celsus Polemaeanus.

[15] *The History of the Christian Religion and Church, During the Three First Centuries*, by Augustus Neander; translated from the German by Henry John Rose, 1848, p. 41

have known out of almost a million at the time of his writing? Moreover, although not highly educated in schools, it **need not** be assumed that most or all of the early Christians were truly illiterate, but that they could read and write (with difficulty).

Let us return to Peter and John. We will assume for the sake of argument that literacy was between five and ten percent, with most readers being men. We will accept that Peter and John were illiterate in the sense the modern historian believes it to be true (even though they likely were not). The time of the statement in Acts about the two apostles' being **"uneducated"** (i.e., unlettered) was about 33 C.E.[16] Peter would not pen his first letter for about 30 more years. Throughout those 30 years, Peter progressed spiritually, maturing into the position of being one of the leaders of the entire first-century Christian congregation. A few years later, Peter and John were viewed as developing and growing into their new position, as leaders in the Jerusalem congregation; as Paul said of them, "James and Cephas and John, who seemed to be pillars" of the Christian community. John, on the other hand, did not pen his books until about 60 years after Acts 4:13. Are we to assume that he too had not grown in 60 years? Could education in the first century have become more accessible?

After the conquests of Alexander the Great and the extension of Macedonian rule in the fourth-century B.C.E., a transferal of people from Greece proper to the small Greek communities in the Middle East took place. Throughout what became known as the Hellenistic period, the Attic dialect, spoken by the educated classes as well as by the traders and many settlers, became the language common to all the Middle East. From about 300 B.C.E. to about 500 C.E. was the age of Koine, or common Greek, a combination of divergent Greek dialects of which Attic was the most significant. Koine soon became the universal language. It had a tremendous advantage over the other languages of this period, in that it was almost universally used. "Koine" means the "common" language, or dialect common to all. The Greek vocabulary of the Old Testament translation, the

---

[16] B.C.E. means "before the Common Era," which is more accurate than B.C. ("before Christ"). C.E. denotes "Common Era," often called A.D., for *anno Domini*, meaning "in the year of our Lord."

47

Septuagint, was the Koine of Alexandria, Egypt, from 280 to 150 B.C.E. Everett Ferguson writes,

> Literacy became more general, and education spread. Both abstract thought and practical intelligence were enhanced in a greater proportion of the population. This change coincided with the spread of Greek language and ideas, so that the level and extent of communication and intelligibility became significant. (Ferguson 2003, 14)

> Education was voluntary, but elementary schools at least were widespread. The indications, especially on the evidence of the papyri, are that the literacy rate of Hellenistic and early Roman times was rather high, probably higher than at any period prior to modern times. Girls as well as boys were often included in the elementary schools, and although education for girls was rarer than for boys, it could be obtained. The key for everyone was to get what you could on your own. (Ferguson 2003, 111)

By the time we enter the first-century C.E., the era of Jesus and the apostles, Koine Greek had become the international language of the Roman Empire. The Bible itself bears witness to this; e.g. when Jesus was executed by the Roman Pontius Pilate, the inscription above his head was in Aramaic, the language of the Jews, in Latin, the official language of Rome, and in Greek, which was the language spoken from the streets of Alexandria, to Jerusalem, to Athens, to Rome and the rest of the empire. (John 19:19, 20; Acts 6:1) Acts 9:29 informs us that Paul was preaching in Jerusalem to Greek-speaking Jews. As we know, Koine, a well-developed tongue by the first-century C.E., would be the tool that would facilitate the publishing of the 27 New Testament books.

The Place of Writing

When we think of the apostle Paul penning his books that would make up most of the New Testament, some have had the anachronistic tendency to impose their modern way of thinking about him, such as presupposing where he would have written.

As I am writing this page, I am tucked away in my home office, seeking privacy from the hustle and bustle of our modern world. This was not the case in the ancient world where Paul lived and traveled. People of that time favored a group setting, not isolation. The apostle Paul probably would have been of this mindset. Paul would not have necessarily sought a quiet place to pen his letters, to escape the noise of those around him. As for myself, I struggle to get back on track if I am interrupted for more than a couple of minutes.

Most during Paul's day would have been surprised by this way of thinking, i.e. seeking quiet and solitude to focus all of one's energy on the task of writing. Those of Paul's day, including himself, would not have even noticed people talking around them, nor would they have been troubled by what we perceive as interruptions, such as the discussions of others, which were neither relevant nor applicable to the subject of their letter writing.

The Scribe of the New Testament Writer

Ancient Greco-Roman society employed secretaries or scribes for various reasons. Of course, the government employed some scribes, working for chief administrators. Then, there were the scribes who were employed in the private sector. These latter scribes (often slaves) usually were employed by the wealthy. However, even high-ranking slaves and freed slaves employed scribes. Many times one would find scribes who would pen letters for their friends. According to E. Randolph Richards, the skills of these unofficial secretaries "could range from a minimal competency with the language and/or the mechanics of writing to the highest proficiency at rapidly producing an accurate, proper, and charming letter."[17] Scribes carried out a wide range of administrative, secretarial, and literary tasks, including administrative bookkeeping, shorthand and taking dictation, letter-writing, and copying literary texts.

The most prominent ways that a scribe would have been used in the first century C.E. would have been as (1) a recorder,

---

[17] (Richards, The Secretary in the Letters of Paul 1990, 11)

(2) an editor, and (3) as a secretary for an author. At the very bottom of the writing tasks, he would be used to record information, i.e. as a record keeper. The New Testament scribes, when they were needed or desired, were being used as secretaries, writing down letters by dictation. Tertius, in taking down the book of Romans with its 7,000+ words, would have simply written out the very words that the apostle Paul spoke. Some have argued that longhand in dictation was not feasible in ancient times because the author would have to slow down to the point of speaking syllable-by-syllable. They usually cite Cicero as evidence for this argument because of the numerous references to dictation in his writings. Cicero stated in a letter to his friend Varro that he had to slow down his dictation to the point of "syllable by syllable" for the sake of the scribe. However, the scribe he was using at that time was inexperienced, not his regular scribe. Of course, it would be very difficult to retain one's line of thought in such a dictation process. It should be noted that Cicero had experienced scribes who could take down dictation at a normal pace of speaking, even rapid speech.[18] Therefore, since there is evidence that there were scribes in those days who were skilled enough to take down dictation at the normal rate of speech, we should not assume that the apostles would not have had access to such scribes in the persons of Tertius, Silvanus, or even Timothy.

In fact, Marcus Fabius Quintilianus (b. 35 C.E. d. 100 C.E.) complained that a scribe who could write at the speed of normal speech can lead to the speaker feeling rushed, to the point of not having time to ponder his thoughts.

> On the other hand, there is a fault which is precisely the opposite of this, into which those fall who insist on first making a rapid draft of their subject with the utmost speed of which their pen is capable, and write in the heat and impulse of the moment. They call this their rough copy. They then revise what they have written, and arrange their hasty outpourings. But while the words and the rhythm may

---

[18] (Richards, Paul And First-Century Letter Writing: Secretaries, Composition and Collection 2004, 29-30); Murphy-O'Connor, *Paul the Letter-Writer*, 9–11; Shorthand references Plutarch, *Cato Minor*, 23.3–5; Caesar, 7.4–5; Seneca, *Epistles*, 14.208.

be corrected, the matter is still marked by the superficiality resulting from the speed with which it was thrown together. The more correct method is, therefore, to exercise care from the very beginning, and to form the work from the outset in such a manner that it merely requires being chiseled into shape, not fashioned anew. Sometimes, however, we must follow the stream of our emotions since their warmth will give us more than any diligence can secure. The condemnation which I have passed on such carelessness in writing will make it pretty clear what my views are on the luxury of dictation which is now so fashionable. For, when we write, however great our speed, the fact that the hand cannot follow the rapidity of our thoughts gives us time to think, whereas the presence of our amanuensis hurries us on, and at times we feel ashamed to hesitate or pause, or make some alteration, as though we were afraid to display such weakness before a witness. As a result, our language tends not merely to be haphazard and formless, but in our desire to produce a continuous flow we let slip positive improprieties of diction, which show neither the precision of the writer nor the impetuosity of the speaker. Again, if the amanuensis is a slow writer or lacking in intelligence, he becomes a stumbling-block, our speed is checked, and the thread of our ideas is interrupted by the delay or even perhaps by the loss of temper to which it gives rise.[19]

Therefore, again, we do have evidence that some scribes were capable, skilled to the point of writing at the normal speed of speech. While Richards says that this is by way of shorthand, saying it was more widespread than originally thought, where the secretary uses symbols in place of words, forming a rough draft that would be written out fully,[20] this need not be the case. True, there is some evidence that shorthand existed a hundred years before Christ. However, it was still rare, with few scribes having the ability. Whether this was true of the scribes that assisted our New Testament authors is an unknown. It is highly unlikely but not necessarily impossible.

---

[19] Institutio Oratoria, 10.3.17–21

[20] (Richards, Paul And First-Century Letter Writing: Secretaries, Composition and Collection 2004, 72)

Who in the days of the New Testament authors would use the services of scribes? Foremost would be those who did not know how to read and write. Within ancient contracts and business letters, one can find a note by the scribe (illiteracy statement), who penned it, stating he had done so because his employer could not read or write. For example, an ancient letter concludes with, "Eumelus, son of Herma, has written for him because he does not know letters."[21] It may be that they were able to read, but struggled with writing. Then again, it may simply be that they wrote slowly, and were not willing to spend the time on improving their skills. An ancient letter from Thebes, Egypt, penned for a certain Asklepiades, concludes, "Written for him hath Eumelus the son of Herma ..., being desired so to do for that he writeth somewhat slowly." (Deissmann 1910, 166-7)

On the other hand, whether one knew how to read and write was not always the decisive issue in the use of a secretary. John L. McKenzie writes, "Even people who could read and write did not think of submitting their readers to unprofessional penmanship. It was probably not even a concern for legibility, but rather a concern for beauty, or at least for neatness," (McKenzie 1975, 14) which moved the ancients to turn to the services of a secretary. Although the educated could read and write, some likely very well, writing was tedious, trying, and frustrating, particularly where lengthy and elaborate texts were concerned. It seems that if one could avoid the tremendous task of penning a lengthy letter, entrusting it to a scribe, so much the better.

The apostle Paul had over 100 traveling companions; like Aristarchus, Luke and Timothy served by the apostle's side for many years. Then, there are others such as Asyncritus, Hermas, Julia, or Philologus, of whom we barely know more than their names. Many of Paul's friends traveled for the sake of the gospel, such as Achaicus, Fortunatus, Stephanas, Artemas, and Tychicus. We know that Tychicus was used by Paul to carry at least three letters now included in the Bible canon: the epistles to the Ephesians, the Colossians, and to Philemon. Tychicus was not

---

[21] See examples in Francis Exler, *The Form of the Ancient Greek Letter: A Study In Greek Epistolography* (Washington D.C.: Catholic University of America, 1922), pp. 126-7

simply some mail carrier. He was a well-trusted carrier for the apostle, Paul. The final greeting from Paul to the Colossians reads,

Colossians 4:7-8 New American Standard Bible (NASB)

⁷ As to all my affairs, Tychicus, *our* beloved brother and faithful servant and fellow bond-servant in the Lord, will bring you information. ⁸ *For* I have sent him to you for this very purpose, that you may know about our circumstances and that he may encourage your hearts;

Richards offers the following about a letter carrier, saying he "was often a personal link between the author and the recipients in addition to the written link. . . . [One purpose] for needing a trustworthy carrier was, he often carried additional information. A letter may describe a situation briefly, frequently with the author's assessment, but the carrier is expected to elaborate for the recipient all the details." (Richards, The Secretary in the Letters of Paul 1990, 7) Many of Paul's letters deal with teachings, as well as one crisis after another; the carrier was expected to be aware of these on a much deeper level so that he could orally explain, and answer any questions. Therefore, he needed to be a highly trusted messenger who was literate.

Tertius was the scribe Paul used to pen his letter to the Romans. We cannot assume that all of Paul's companions were proficient readers and writers, but we can infer that Paul would task coworkers, who were able to carry and read letters, as well as understand the condition of the people or congregation where they were being sent or stationed. In addition, the scribes whom Paul used, such as Tertius, would very likely have been semi-professional or professional. It would have been simply senseless to entrust the secretarial work of taking down the monumental words of the book of Romans, for example, to an inexperienced scribe. What skills would Tertius need to carry out the task of penning the book of Romans?

The ordinary coworker of Paul would likely have been able to read proficiently, but barely be able to write. Paul would have chosen workers whose skills would have equipped them to carry out their assignments. Tertius would have been the exception to the rule, most likely having been a professional scribe. He would have to have been able to glue the sheets together if it was to be a roll or stitch the pages together if a codex. He would need to know the appropriate mixture of soot and gum to make ink and to be able to use his knife to make his own reed pen. Richards writes that a professional scribe would also "draw lines on the paper. Small holes were often pricked down each side, and then a straight edge and a lead disk were used to lightly draw evenly spaced lines across the sheet."[22] If Tertius had not been trained as a copyist of documents, he would have made many minor errors because his attention would have been on the sense of what he was penning, as opposed to the exact words, as is typical of the unconscious mind.

Did Tertius take Paul's exact dictation, word for word? Robert H. Mounce writes,

> The only legitimate question about authorship relates to the role of Tertius, who in 16:22 writes, 'I Tertius, who wrote down this letter, greet you in the Lord.' We know that at that time in history an amanuensis [scribe] that is, one hired to write from dictation, could serve at several levels. In some cases, he would receive dictation and write it down immediately in longhand. At other times, he might use a form of shorthand (*tachygraphy* [ancient shorthand]) to take down a letter and then later write it out in longhand. In some cases, an amanuensis would simply get the gist of what a person wanted to say and then be left on his own to formulate the ideas into a letter. (R. H. Mounce 2001, 22)

It might seem quite the task for Tertius to take down Paul's words in longhand. However, this is not to say that it was impossible, just difficult. Paul might have had to speak in a slow to a normal rate of speech, **but not** syllable-by-syllable. It is true that Tertius would have been writing on a papyrus sheet with a reed pen, with the intention of being legible; however, he would have been very skilled in his trade. Then again, there is the slight possibility of Tertius taking it down in shorthand and thereafter making out a full draft, which would have been reviewed by

---

[22] (Richards, Paul And First-Century Letter Writing: Secretaries, Composition and Collection 2004, 29)

both Paul and Tertius. The last option by Mounce in the above is contrary to the attitudes that both the scribes and the New Testament authors would have had toward what was being penned. God chose to convey a message through Matthew, Mark, Luke, John, Peter, Jude, James, and Paul, not Tertius and Silvanus, or others. We cannot say with any certainty whether Tertius or Silvanus took their authors' words down in shorthand or longhand. We can say, however, that the Word of God was being dictated by the human author to the scribe, and in no way composed by the scribe.

Inspiration and Inerrancy in the Writing Process

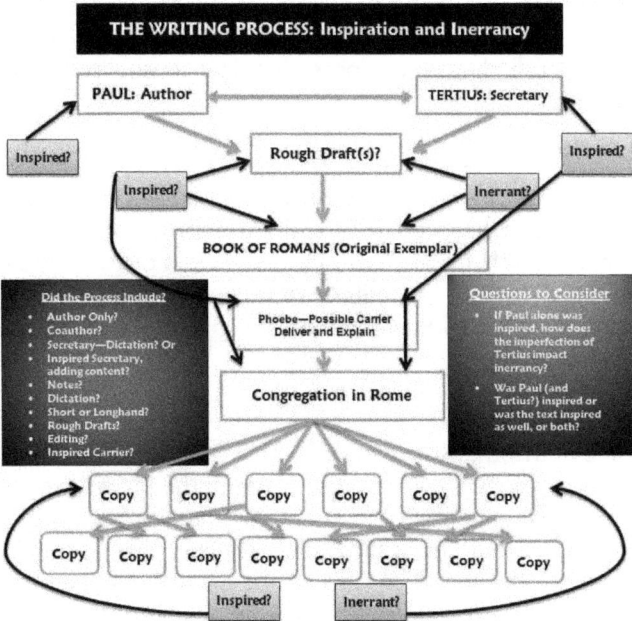

THE WRITING PROCESS: Inspiration and Inerrancy

All Scripture is Inspired by God

In this context, inspiration is **the state** of a human being moved by the Holy Spirit, which results in an inspired, fully inerrant written Word of God.

Chicago Statement on Biblical Inerrancy ICBI (Bold mine)

Article VII

We affirm that **inspiration** was the work in which God by His Spirit, through human writers, gave us His Word. The origin of Scripture is divine. The mode of divine **inspiration** remains largely a mystery to us. We deny that **inspiration** can be reduced to human insight, or to heightened states of consciousness of any kind.

Article VIII

We affirm that God in His Work of **inspiration** utilized the distinctive personalities and literary styles of the writers whom He had chosen and prepared. We deny that God, in causing these writers to use the very words that He chose, overrode their personalities.

Article IX

We affirm that **inspiration**, though not conferring omniscience, guaranteed true and trustworthy utterance on all matters of which the Biblical authors were moved to speak and write. We deny that the finitude or fallenness of these writers, by necessity or otherwise, introduced distortion or falsehood into God's Word.

Article X

We affirm that **inspiration**, strictly speaking, applies only to the autographic text of Scripture, which in the providence of God can be ascertained from available manuscripts with great accuracy. We further affirm that copies and translations of Scripture are the Word of God to the extent that they faithfully represent the original. We deny that any essential element of the Christian faith is affected by the absence of the autographs. We further deny that this absence renders the assertion of Biblical **inerrancy** invalid or irrelevant.

Article XI

We affirm that Scripture, having been given by divine inspiration, is infallible, so that, far from misleading us, it is true and reliable in all the matters it addresses. We deny that it is possible for the Bible to be at the same time infallible and errant in its assertions. Infallibility and inerrancy may be distinguished, but not separated.

Inerrancy of Scripture

Inerrancy of Scripture is **the result** of the state of a human being moved by Holy Spirit from God, which results in an inspired, fully inerrant written Word of God.

Article XII

We affirm that Scripture in its entirety is **inerrant**, being free from all falsehood, fraud, or deceit. We deny that Biblical infallibility and **inerrancy** are limited to spiritual, religious, or redemptive themes, exclusive of assertions in the fields of history and science. We further deny that scientific hypotheses about earth history may properly be used to overturn the teaching of Scripture on creation and the flood.

Article XIII

We affirm the propriety of using **inerrancy** as a theological term with reference to the complete truthfulness of Scripture. We deny that it is proper to evaluate Scripture according to standards of truth and error that are alien to its usage or purpose. We further deny that **inerrancy** is negated by Biblical phenomena such as a lack of modern technical precision, irregularities of grammar or spelling, observational descriptions of nature, the reporting of falsehoods, the use of hyperbole and round numbers, the topical arrangement of material, variant selections of material in parallel accounts, or the use of free citations.

Article XV

We affirm that the doctrine of **inerrancy** is grounded in the teaching of the Bible about **inspiration**. We deny that Jesus' teaching about Scripture may be dismissed by appeals to accommodation or to any natural limitation of His humanity.

Article XVI

We affirm that the doctrine of **inerrancy** has been integral to the Church's faith throughout its history. We deny that inerrancy is a doctrine invented by Scholastic Protestantism, or is a reactionary position postulated in response to negative higher criticism.

Authoritative Word of God

The **authoritative** aspect of Scripture is that God by way of inspiration gives the words the authors chose to use power and authority, so that the outcome (i.e., originals) is the very Word of God, as though God were speaking to us himself.

Article I

We affirm that the Holy Scriptures are to be received as the **authoritative** Word of God. We deny that the Scriptures receive their authority from the Church, tradition, or any other human source.

2 Timothy 3:16-17 New American Standard Bible (NASB)

¹⁶ All Scripture is inspired by God and profitable for teaching, for reproof, for correction, for training in righteousness; ¹⁷ so that the man of God may be adequate, equipped for every good work.

What does this mean? The phrase "inspired by God" (Gr., *theopneustos*) literally means, "Breathed out by God." A related Greek word, *pneuma*, means "wind," "breath," life, "Spirit." Since *pneuma* can also mean "breath," the process of "breathing out" can rightly be said to be the work of the Holy Spirit inspiring the Scriptures. The result is that the originals were accurate, fully inerrant and authoritative. Thus the Holy Spirit moved human writers so that the result can truthfully be called the Word of God, not the word of man.

2 Peter 1:21 New American Standard Bible (NASB)

²¹ for no prophecy was ever made by an act of human will, but men moved by the Holy Spirit spoke from God.

The Greek word here translated "men moved by (NASB)," *phero*, is used in another form at Acts 27:15, 17, which describes a ship that was driven along by the wind. So the Holy Spirit, by analogy, 'navigated the course' of the Bible writers. While the

Spirit did not give them each word by dictation,[23] it certainly kept the writers from inserting any information that did not convey the will and purpose of God.

The heart of what the International Council on Biblical Inerrancy (ICBI) stood for is apparent in "A Short Statement," produced at the Chicago conference in 1978:

A SHORT STATEMENT

1. God, who is Himself Truth and speaks truth only, has inspired Holy Scripture in order thereby to reveal Himself to lost mankind through Jesus Christ as Creator and Lord, Redeemer and Judge. Holy Scripture is God's witness to Himself.

2. Holy Scripture, being God's own Word, written by men prepared and superintended by His Spirit, is of infallible divine authority in all matters upon which it touches: it is to be believed, as God's instruction, in all that it affirms, obeyed, as God's command, in all that it requires; embraced, as God's pledge, in all that it promises.

3. The Holy Spirit, Scripture's divine Author, both authenticates it to us by His inward witness and opens our minds to understand its meaning.

4. Being wholly and verbally God-given, Scripture is without error or fault in all its teaching, no less in what it states about God's acts in creation, about the events of world history, and about its own literary origins under God, than in its witness to God's saving grace in individual lives.

5. The **authority of Scripture** is inescapably impaired if this total divine **inerrancy** is in any way limited or disregarded, or made relative to a view of truth contrary to the Bible's own; and such lapses bring serious loss to both the individual and the Church.

Questions to Consider

---

[23] Exactly how the Spirit guided the writers is a mystery, and the words "thus says the Lord" in prophecy most likely do introduce a dictated message. However, those familiar with Greek can easily see stylistic differences between the NT writers, which seem to reflect different personalities, and rule out verbatim dictation from a single source.

We have been using the book of Romans as our example, so we will continue with it. We know that Paul was the author who gave us the inspired content of Romans, Tertius was the secretary who recorded Romans, and Phoebe was likely the one who carried the letter to Rome or else accompanied the one who did. Thus, we have at least three persons: the author, the secretary (scribe), and the carrier.

What is inspiration?

Inspiration is a "theological concept encompassing phenomena in which human action, skill, or utterance is immediately and extraordinarily supplied by the Spirit of God. Although various terms are employed in the Bible, the basic meaning is best served by Gk. *theopneustos* "God-breathed" (2 Tim. 3:16), meaning "breathed forth by God" rather than "breathed into by God" (Warfield)." (Myers 1987, 524) **Verbal plenary inspiration** holds that "every word of Scripture was God-breathed." A significant role was played by the human writers. Their individual backgrounds, personal traits, and literary styles were authentically theirs, but had been providentially prepared by God for use as his instrument in producing Scripture. "The Scriptures had not been dictated, but the result was as if they had been (A. A. Hodge, B. B. Warfield)." (Myers 1987, 525)

Benjamin B. Warfield: "Inspiration is, therefore, usually defined as a supernatural influence exerted on the sacred writers by the Spirit of God, by virtue of which their writings are given Divine trustworthiness."[24]

Edward J. Young: "Inspiration is a superintendence of God the Holy Spirit over the writers of the Scriptures, as a result of which these Scriptures possess Divine authority and trustworthiness and, possessing such Divine authority and trustworthiness, are free from error."[25]

Charles C. Ryrie: "Inspiration is ... God's superintendence of the human authors so that, using their own individual

---

[24] B. B. Warfield, *The Inspiration and Authority of the Bible*(Philadelphia: Presbyterian and Reformed, 1948), p. 131.

[25] Edward J. Young, *Thy Word Is Truth* (Grand Rapids: Eerdmans, 1957), p. 27.

personalities, they composed and recorded without error His revelation to man in the words of the original autographs."[26]

Paul P. Enns: "There are several important elements that belong in a proper definition of inspiration: (1) the divine element—God the Holy Spirit superintended the writers, ensuring the accuracy of the writing; (2) the human element—human authors wrote according to their individual styles and personalities; (3) the result of the divine-human authorship is the recording of God's truth without error; (4) inspiration extends to the selection of words by the writers; (5) inspiration relates to the original manuscripts."[27]

Were both Paul and Tertius inspired, or just Paul?

Only Paul and other Old and New Testament authors were inspired. First, as was stated above, **Verbal plenary inspiration** holds that "every word of Scripture was God-breathed." God **did not**, generally speaking, dictate the books of the Bible word by word to the Bible authors as if they were dictating machines.

2 Thessalonians 3:17 New American Standard Bible (NASB)

[17] I, Paul, write this greeting with my own hand, and this is a distinguishing mark in every letter; this is the way I write.

An appended note to every letter with his signature "distinguishing mark" is like a boss signing a letter that he dictated to a secretary. It is unthinkable that Paul would sign or make a distinguishing mark on anything without reading through it and make any necessary corrections. This supposes that Paul looked over all of his letters, which would also suppose that the scribe could not have been inspired because if he were, then there would have been no mistakes in the document, which means it would not have been needed to be looked over let alone corrected. So again, there would have been no need for Paul to check the work of an inspired secretary. If Tertius had been

---

[26] Charles C. Ryrie, *A Survey of Bible Doctrine* (Chicago: Moody, 1972), p. 38.

[27] Paul P. Enns, *The Moody Handbook of Theology* (Chicago: Moody Press, 1989), p. 161.

inspired, the moment he sat the pen down, Paul would have had no need to look the text over. There is no need to read into silence and suggest that the secretary was inspired. While the secretary was certainly engaged in his work being that they were coworkers and traveling companions,

However, in some cases, information was transmitted by verbal dictation, word for word. For example, when God delivered the large body of laws and statutes of his covenant with Israel, Jehovah instructed Moses: "Write for yourself these words." (Ex 34:27, LEB) In another example, the prophets were often given specific messages to deliver. (1 Ki 22:14; Jer. 1:7; 2:1; 11:1-5; Eze. 3:4; 11:5) More importantly, the Bible authors did dictate what they received under inspiration to their secretaries, i.e., amanuenses/scribes.

Jeremiah 36:4 New American Standard Bible (NASB)

⁴ Then Jeremiah called Baruch the son of Neriah, and Baruch wrote on a scroll at **the dictation of Jeremiah** all the words of the Lord which He had spoken to him. (Bold mine)

If Paul alone was inspired, how does the imperfection of Tertius affect inerrancy?

First, we should state that just because Paul used Tertius, Peter used Silvanus, or Jeremiah used Baruch, to pen the Word of God, they did not thereby detract from or weaken the authority of God's Word or the inerrancy of Scripture. The dictation that Paul gave Tertius was the result of divine inspiration as he, Paul, was moved along by Holy Spirit. Tertius merely recorded Paul's dictation, word by word. Whether Tertius was a professional scribe[28] or had the skills of a semi-professional scribe, he must have made at least a few slips of the pen. Afterward, however, Paul would have reviewed the document with Tertius, correcting any errors before publishing the official, authoritative text.

What about Phoebe, what role did the carrier have in the process?

---

[28] In the strictest sense, a professional scribe is one who was specifically trained in that vocation and was paid for his services.

Those used by New Testament authors to deliver the Word of God to people or congregations would have been some of Paul's most trusted, competent coworkers. Certainly, in the case of congregations contacting Paul with questions and concerns, to which Paul responded with an inspired letter, the carrier would be made aware of those questions and concerns. Paul would have spoken to the carrier at length about these matters, going over what he meant by what he wrote. This would have provided the carrier sufficient knowledge, in case the person or congregation had any question that the carrier could address. This process is not indicated within the Scriptures; but are we to believe God and Paul for that matter would send a simple carrier who was left in the dark as to what he was carrying, and that no congregational leader would have follow-up questions, which God would have foreseen? Hardly.

The Publishing, Copying and Distributing Process

In the above, we spoke of the initial aspect of the publishing process, i.e., the moment Paul decided to pen a letter to a congregation like the Romans, the Ephesians, the Colossians, or to a person such as Philemon. We discussed the process that Paul went through with his secretary (e.g., Tertius), to the carrier (e.g., Phoebe, Tychicus) and the recipients. Now we turn to the circulation aspect, i.e., getting the book out to more and more readers. Harry Y. Gamble says the following in *The Publication and Early Dissemination of Early Christian Books*:

> The letters of Paul to his communities, the earliest extant Christian texts, were dictated to scribal associates (presumably Christian), carried to their destinations by a traveling Christian, and read aloud to the congregations.[29] But Paul also envisioned the circulation

---

[29] On the dictation of Paul's letters to a scribe, see E. R. Richards, The Secretary in the Letters of Paul (WUNT 42; Tubingen: Mohr, 1991), 169–98; for couriers see Rom. 16: 1, 1 Cor. 16: 10, Eph. 6: 21, Col. 4: 7, cf. 2 Cor. 8: 16–17. Reference to their carriers is common in other early Christian letters (e.g. 1 Pet. 5: 12, 1 Clem. 65: 1, Ignatius, Phil. 11.2, Smyr. 12.1, Polycarp, Phil. 14.1). For the general practice see E. Epp, 'New Testament Papyrus Manuscripts and Letter Carrying in Greco-Roman Times', in B. A. Pearson (ed.), The Future of Early Christianity (Minneapolis: Fortress, 1991), 35–56. Reading a letter aloud to the

of some of his letters beyond a single Christian group (cf. Gal. 1: 2, 'to the churches of Galatia', Rom. 1:7 'to all God's beloved in Rome'—dispersed among numerous discrete house churches, Rom. 16: 5, 10, 11, 14, 15), and the author of Colossians, if not Paul, gives instruction for the exchange of Paul's letters between different communities (Col. 4: 16), which must indeed have taken place also soon after Paul's time.[30] The gospel literature of early Christianity offers only meager hints of intentions or means of its publication and circulation. The prologue to Luke/Acts (Luke 1: 1–4) provides a dedication to 'Theophilus', who (whether or not a fictive figure) by that convention is implicitly made responsible for the dissemination of the work by encouraging and permitting copies to be made. The last chapter of the Gospel of John, an epilogue added by others after the original conclusion of the Gospel (20: 30–1), aims at least in part (21: 24–5) to insure appreciation of the book and to promote its use beyond its community of origin. To take another case, the Apocalypse, addressed to seven churches in western Asia Minor, was almost surely sent in separate copy to each. Even so, the author anticipated its wider copying and dissemination beyond those original recipients, and so warned subsequent copyists to preserve the integrity of the book, neither adding nor subtracting, for fear of religious penalty (Rev. 22: 18–19). The private Christian copying and circulation that is presumed in these early writings continued to be the means for the publication and dissemination of Christian literature in the second and third centuries. It can be seen, for example, in the explicit notice in The Shepherd of Hermas (Vis. 2.4.3) that the book was to be published or released in two final copies, one for local use in Rome, the other for the transcription of further copies to be sent to Christian

---

community, which seems to be presupposed by all the letters, is stipulated only in 1 Thess. 5: 27.

[30] This is shown for an early time by the generalization of the original particular addresses of some of Paul's letters (Rom. 1: 7, 15; 1 Cor. 1: 2; cf. Eph. 1: 1).

communities in 'cities abroad'. It can also be seen when Polycarp, bishop of Smyrna, had the letters of Ignatius copied and sent to the Christian community in Philippi, and had copies of letters from them and other churches in Asia Minor sent to Syrian Antioch (Phil. 13). It is evident too in the scribal colophons of the Martyrdom of Polycarp (22.2–4), and must be assumed also in connection with the letters of Dionysius, bishop of Corinth (fl. 170 ce; Eusebius, H.E. 4.23.1–12).

From another angle, the physical remains of early Christian books show that they were produced and disseminated privately within and between Christian communities. Early Christian texts, especially those of a scriptural sort, were almost always written in codices or leaf books—an informal, economical, and handy format—rather than on rolls, which were the traditional and standard vehicle of all other books. This was a sharp departure from convention, and particularly characteristic of Christians. Also distinctive to Christian books was the pervasive use of nomina sacra, divine names written in abbreviated forms, which was clearly an in-house practice of Christian scribes. Further, the preponderance in early Christian papyrus manuscripts of an informal quasi-documentary script rather than a professional bookhand also suggests that Christian writings were privately transcribed with a view to intramural circulation and use.[31]

If Christian books were disseminated in roughly the same way as other books, that is, by private seriatim copying, we might surmise that they spread slowly and gradually in ever-widening circles, first in proximity to their places of origin, then regionally, and then transregionally, and for some books this was doubtless the case. But it deserves notice that some early Christian texts appear to have enjoyed surprisingly rapid and wide circulation. Already by the early

---

[31] On these features see H. Gamble, Books and Readers in the Early Church (New Haven: Yale University Press, 1995), 66–81, and L. Hurtado, The Earliest Christian Artifacts (Grand Rapids: Eerdmans, 2006).

decades of the second century Papias of Hierapolis in western Asia Minor was acquainted at least with the Gospels of Mark and Matthew (Eusebius, H.E. 3.39.15–16); Clement of Rome, Ignatius of Antioch, and Polycarp of Smyrna were all acquainted with collections of Paul's letters; and papyrus copies of various early Christian texts were current in Egypt.[32] The Shepherd of Hermas, written in Rome near the mid-second century, was current and popular in Egypt not long after.[33] Equally interesting, Irenaeus' Adversus haereses, written about 180 in Gaul, is shown by papyrus fragments to have found its way to Egypt by the end of the second century, and indeed also to Carthage, where it was used by Tertullian.[34]

The brisk and broad dissemination of Christian books presumes not only a lively interest in texts among Christian communities but also efficient means for their reproduction and distribution. Such interest and means may be unexpected, given that the rate of literacy within Christianity was low, on average no greater than in the empire at large, namely in the range of 10–15 percent.[35] Yet there were some literate members in almost all Christian communities, and as long as texts could be read aloud by some, they were accessible and useful to the illiterate majority. Christian

---

[32] For Clement, Ignatius, and Polycarp, see A. F. Gregory and C. M. Tuckett, eds., The Reception of the New Testament in the Apostolic Fathers (Oxford: OUP, 2005), 142–53, 162–72, 201–18, 226–7. For early Christian papyri in Egypt see Hurtado, Earliest Christian Artifacts, appendix 1 (209–29). The most notable case is P52 (a fragment of the Gospel of John, customarily dated to the early 2nd cent.).

[33] Some papyrus fragments of Hermas are 2nd cent. (P.Oxy. 4706 and 3528, P.Mich. 130, P.Iand. 1.4).

[34] For the A.H. in Egypt: P.Oxy. 405; for Tertullian's use of A.H. in Carthage, see T. D. Barnes, Tertullian (Oxford: Clarendon, 1971), 127–8, 220–1.

[35] The fundamental study of literacy in antiquity is still W. V. Harris, Ancient Literacy (Cambridge, Mass.: Harvard University Press, 1989); see now also the essays in J. H. Humphrey, ed., Literacy in the Roman World (Journal of Roman Archaeology, suppl. ser. 3; Ann Arbor: University of Michigan, 1991), and in W. A. Johnson and H. N. Parker, eds., Ancient Literacies (Oxford: OUP, 2009).

congregations were not reading communities in the same sense as elite literary or scholarly circles, but books were nevertheless important to them virtually from the beginning, for even before Christians began to compose their own texts, books of Jewish scripture played an indispensable role in their worship, teaching, and missionary preaching. Indeed, Judaism and Christianity were the only religious communities in Greco-Roman antiquity in which texts had any considerable importance, and in this, as in some other respects, Christian groups bore a greater resemblance to philosophical circles than to other religious traditions.[36]

If smaller, provincial Christian congregations were not well-equipped or well-situated for the tasks of copying and disseminating texts, larger Christian centers must have had some scriptorial capacity: already in the second century: Polycarp's handling of Ignatius' letters and letters from other churches shows its presence in Smyrna; the instruction about the publication of Hermas' The Shepherd suggests it for Rome; and it can hardly be doubted for Alexandria, since even in a provincial city like Oxyrhynchus many manuscripts of Christian texts were available.[37] The early third-century Alexandrian scriptorium devised for the production and distribution of the works of Origen (Eusebius, H.E. 6.23.2), though unique in its sponsorship by a private patron and its service to an individual writer, surely had precursors, more modest and yet efficient, in other Christian communities. It also had important successors,

---

[36] M. Beard, 'Writing and Religion: Ancient Religion and the Function of the Written Word in Roman Religion', in Humphrey, Literacy in the Roman World, 353–8, argues that texts played a relatively large role in Greco-Roman religions, yet characterizes that role as 'symbolic rather than utilitarian', which was clearly not the case in early Christianity. The kind of careful reading, interpretation, and exposition of texts that we see in early Christianity and in early Judaism (whether in worship or school settings) provides, mutatis mutandis, an interesting analogy to the activity of elite literary circles.

[37] On the question of early Christian scriptoria (the term may be variously construed), see Gamble, Books and Readers, 121–6. Hurtado, Earliest Christian Artifacts, 185–9, rightly calls attention to corrections by contemporary hands in early Christian papyri as pointing to at least limited activity of a scriptorial kind.

not the least of which was the library and scriptorium that flourished in Caesarea in the second half of the third century under the auspices of Pamphilus.[38] Absent such reliable intra-Christian means for the production of books, the range of texts known and used by Christian communities across the Mediterranean basin by the end of the second century would be without explanation.[39]
(Hill and Kruger 2012, 32-35)

When we think of publishing a book today, there are some similarities to the ancient process, but of course, it was not the same for Christian communities in the ancient world of the Roman Empire. Paul dispatched Tychicus as a carrier with a letter to the Ephesians, to the Colossians, and to Philemon, as well as a potential fourth letter to the Laodiceans. Tychicus was a competent, trusted, skilled coworker, who delivered these letters hundreds of miles from an imprisoned Paul, with enough information to bring God's Word to the first-century Christian congregations. However, in the letter to the Colossians, Paul said, "When this letter has been read among you, have it also read in the church of the Laodiceans; and see that you also read the letter from Laodicea." (Col. 4:16) In other words, it was to be a circuit letter. Paul had also stated to the Thessalonians in a letter to them, "I put you under oath before the Lord to have this letter read to all the brothers." (1 Thess. 5:27) Paul encouraged the distribution of his books.

Remember the process from the above; the book would be shared with friends of similar interests, and then the circles grew wider and wider to friends of friends and others. First, Paul's primary level of friends would be his more than one hundred

---

[38] The role of Pamphilus and the Caesarean library/scriptorium in the private production and dissemination of early Christian literature, esp. of scriptural materials, was highlighted by Eusebius in his Life of Pamphilus, as quoted by Jerome in his Apology against Rufinus (1.9).

[39] Beyond the uses of Christian texts in congregational settings, there were already in the 2nd cent. some Christian circles that pursued specialized and technical engagements with texts, usually in the service of theological arguments and exegetical agendas. The 'school-settings' of teachers such as Valentinus and Justin, and a little later of Theodotus, Clement, and Origen, were Christian approximations to the kinds of literary activity associated with 'elite' reading communities in the early empire.

traveling companions and fellow workers, some being the carriers who delivered the books. Second, the friends in the Christian congregation would have the letter read to them, who would then share it with other fellow congregations. In the secular circle of friends, interested readers who wished to have a copy would have their slaves (i.e., scribes) make a copy or copies of a book. The same would have been true within the Christian congregation. When the Laodiceans read the letter that had been sent by Paul to the Colossians, they would have had one of their wealthy members use his literate and trained scribe to make a copy for their congregation and maybe even a few copies for other members. Now the same would hold true when the Colossians received the letter that had been written to the Laodiceans. Eventually, Paul's letters would be gathered together so that they circulated as a group, such as P[46].

The scriptorium was a room for copying manuscripts, where a lector would read aloud from his exemplar with a room full of copyists taking down his dictation. Recent scholarship has suggested that we remove the concept of the scriptorium in the time of Jesus and the apostles of the first century C.E., on the grounds that this was not a practice until the fourth century C.E. Harry Y. Gamble addresses this effectively when he writes,

> It is difficult to determine just when Christian scriptoria came into existence. The problem is partly of definition, partly of evidence. If we think of the scriptorium as simply a writing center where texts were copied by more than a single scribe, then any of the larger Christian communities, such as Antioch or Rome, may have already had scriptoria in the early second century, and in view of Polycarp's activity something of the kind can be imagined for Smyrna. If we think instead of a scriptorium as being more structured, operating, for example, in a specially designed and designated location; employing particular methods of transcription; producing certain types of manuscripts; or multiplying copies on a significant scale, then it becomes more difficult to imagine that such institutions developed at an early date. (Gamble 1995, 121)

Gamble goes on to inform us that Origen's scriptorium of about 230 C.E. was an exception. The scriptorium of Cyprian just a few short years later was a more official version of what we think of when picturing scriptoria. Then, there is the scriptorium that was attached to the Christian library in Caesarea, which we know was commissioned to produce fifty New Testament manuscripts in short order. It may even have been added in the third century when Pamphilus (latter half of the 3rd century–309 C.E.) built the library. It is likely that a more official type of scriptorium could be found in this period at other Christian epicenters, such as Rome, Jerusalem, and Alexandria. Gamble adds, "It was only during the fourth and fifth centuries that the scriptoria on monastic communities came into their own, also in association with monastic libraries." (Gamble 1995, 121-2)

While it is extremely difficult, if not impossible to identify a specific Alexandrian scriptorium for our early manuscripts of the second century, or even if they were produced in a scriptorium at all, we do know that professional scribes produced them. There are many possibilities: (1) the professional scribe could have produced them in a Christian scriptorium. On the other hand, (2) the professional scribe could have been a Christian who worked for a scriptorium, who then used his skills to produce copies. Then again, (3) it could have been that the scribe formerly worked in a scriptorium, but now was the private scribe of a wealthy Christian, who used his skills to make copies. What we do know is that there were about a million Christians spread throughout the Roman Empire at the beginning of the second century. Therefore, the copying of manuscripts could very well have been within the Christian community, i.e., from Christian congregation to Christian congregation, as well as wealthy Christians acquiring personal copies for themselves.

We have a number of early manuscripts that evidence that they were very likely produced in a scriptorium, even if it was simply a room attached to a Christian library, which had a handful of copyists. For example, P[46] (150 C.E.) was certainly done by a professional scribe because it contained stichoi marks, which are notes at the end of sections, stating how many lines were copied. This was a means of calculating how much a scribe should be paid. It is likely that an employee of the scriptorium numbered the pages, indicating the stichoi marks. Moreover, this same scribe made corrections as he went. Another example would be P[66], according to Comfort:

> It is also fairly certain that P[66] was the product of a scriptorium or writing center. The first copyist of this manuscript had his work thoroughly checked by a diorthotes [corrector], according to a different exemplar—just the way it would happen in a scriptorium. Of course, it can be argued that an individual who purchased the manuscript made all the corrections, which was a common practice in ancient times. But the extent of corrections in P[66] and the fact that the paginator (a different scribe) made many of the corrections speaks against this (see description of P[66] in chap. 2). It was more the exception than the rule in ancient times that a manuscript would be fully checked by a diorthotes. P[66] has other markings of being professionally produced. The extant manuscript still shows the pinpricks in the corners of each leaf of the papyri; these served as a guide for left hand justification and right hand. The manuscript also exhibits a consistent set of marginal and interlinear correction signs. Another sign of professionally produced manuscript is the use of the diple (>) in the margin, which was used to signal a correction in the text and/or the need for a correction in the text. There are very few of these in the extant New Testament manuscripts. (P. W. Comfort 2008, 26)

The production and distribution of New Testament manuscripts were carried out at the congregation and individual Christian level in the early days of Christianity. Moreover, this process did not negate the use of professional scribes. Just as Paul would not have used an inexperienced scribe to produce the book of Romans, congregations and wealthy Christians would have likely used professional scribes to make copies. Of course, there are exceptions to the rule and some congregations may not have had access to a professional scribe, so they would have to have chosen to use the best person available to them. Nevertheless, if a congregation had access to a semi-professional or professional scribe, it would have been a lack of good sense or practicality not to take advantage of such a person. Think of anything we want to have done in our Christian congregation today: would we not seek out a professional, if we had access to one as a member, be it plumbing, wiring, teaching, or computer technology? We naturally look to the most skilled person that we can find even if we have a clogged up a commode. Would we do any less if we were in the first century and had just received a letter from the apostle Paul, who was imprisoned hundreds of miles away in Rome?

Review Questions

- Were the apostle Peter and John uneducated?

- What is inspiration?

- What does the Chicago Statement on Biblical Inerrancy ICBI say on inerrancy?

- How does the Short Statement deal with inspiration and inerrancy?

- What is inspiration and how do different scholars explain it?

- Were both Paul and Tertius inspired, or just Paul?

- If Paul alone was inspired, how does the imperfection of Tertius affect inerrancy?

- What about Phoebe, what role did the carrier have in the process?

CHAPTER 3 Inerrancy

As you may know, there are several different levels of inerrancy. **Absolute Inerrancy** is the belief that the Bible is fully true and exact in every way; including not only relationships and doctrine, but also science and history. In other words, all information is completely exact. **Full Inerrancy** is the belief that the Bible was not written as a science or historical textbook, but is phenomenological, in that it is written from the human perspective. In other words, speaking of such things as the sun rising (still used today), the four corners of the earth (still used today), or the rounding off number approximations are all from a human perspective. **Limited Inerrancy** is the belief that the Bible is meant only as a reflection of God's purposes and will, so the science and history is the understanding of the author's day, and is limited. Thus, the Bible is susceptible to errors in these areas. **Inerrancy of Purpose** is the belief that it is only inerrant in the purpose of bringing its readers to a saving faith. The Bible is not about facts, but about persons and relationships, thus, it is subject to error. Inspired: Not Inerrant is the belief that its authors are human and thus subject to human error. It should be noted that **this author holds the position of _full inerrancy_**.

For many today, the Bible is nothing more than a book written by men, which is full of myths and legends, contradictions, as well as geographical, historical, and scientific errors. University professor Gerald A. Larue had this to say, "The views of the writers as expressed in the Bible reflect the ideas, beliefs, and concepts current in their own times and are limited by the extent of knowledge in those times." (Larue 1983, 39) On the other hand, the Bible's claims are quite different.

2 Timothy 3:16-17 Updated American Standard Version (UASV)

16 All Scripture is inspired by God and profitable for teaching, for reproof, for correction, for training in righteousness; 17 so that the man of God may be fully competent, equipped for every good work.

2 Peter 1:20-21 Updated American Standard Version (UASV)

[20] But know this first, that no prophecy of Scripture comes from one's own interpretation, [21] for no prophecy was ever produced by the will of man, but men carried

Below are two very good examples from the 20th century history of Inerrancy of Scripture, and the pattern of behavior, which has now become the norm. Both examples are from *Defending Inerrancy: Affirming the Accuracy of Scripture for a New Generation*, by Geisler, Norman L.; Roach, Bill (2012).

EXAMPLE ONE

The rift over inerrancy remained simmering on the back burner. Two important factors gave impetus to the limited inerrancy movement (that inerrancy was limited to only redemptive matters). First, neoevangelicalism arose originally from a sermon by Ockenga in 1948 at the Civic Auditorium in Pasadena. It was a call to repudiate separationism and involve evangelicals in social action while retaining a commitment to fundamental doctrines like inerrancy. It was not initially designed as a movement, but the name caught on as it was used by Edward Carnell and Harold Lindsell, and also by Carl Henry (who had already written The Uneasy Conscience of Modern Fundamentalism, 1947); Gleason Archer also began to support it. Soon after this, younger evangelicals started to join the movement, and the doctrinal emphasis was downplayed until inerrancy was no longer a characteristic of the group.

EXAMPLE TWO

According to Harold Lindsell (Battle for the Bible, chap. 6), in 1947 Charles Fuller invited Ockenga to join him in founding a School of Missions and Evangelism. "Biblical inerrancy" was part of the doctrinal statement. Harold Lindsell was the first dean and with Wilbur Smith, Everett F. Harrison, and Carl Henry formed the first faculty. The doctrinal statement of Scripture read: "The books which form the canon of the Old and New Testaments as originally given are plenarily inspired and free from all error in the whole and in the part. These books constitute the written

Word of God, the only infallible rule of faith and practice." Such a statement meant that the Bible is free from errors in matters of fact, science, history, and chronology, as well as in matters having to do with salvation.

Within the ensuing years, doubts began to arise on the Fuller board and faculty about the inerrancy of Scripture. First, Fuller staff member Bela Vassady said his honesty kept him from signing the inerrancy part of the doctrinal statement, and he voluntarily left the school. By 1962 it became apparent that others at Fuller no longer believed in inerrancy. One wealthy and influential board member, C. David Weyerhaeuser, came to the conviction that the Bible was not inerrant. Two other faculty members came to the same conclusion, but neither was asked to leave the school. The founder's son, Daniel Fuller (after studying under Karl Barth in Basel), soon followed suit. Calvin Schoonhoven admitted that he did not believe in inerrancy when he was hired. Finally, David Hubbard was hired as president in spite of the fact that the syllabus on the Old Testament he had coauthored with Robert Laurin stated that Adam was not historical, Moses had not written the whole Pentateuch, and Daniel was written after the great world kingdom events that are recorded as prophecies in his book (though Hubbard maintained that his own views were orthodox).

In December 1962, "Black Saturday" occurred at a faculty-trustee meeting in Pasadena. Here a number of faculty and board members expressed that they did not believe in the inerrancy of Scripture. Edward Johnson declared his belief that inerrancy was a "benchmark" belief and resigned because the board failed to take its stand on inerrancy (which was still in the doctrinal statement from its beginning).

Geisler goes through numerous situations like the above, where good men, with great intentions for a group or school that accepts full or total inerrancy, and over time, member after member begins to abandon the whole purpose of founding the group or school. In the end, the group or school is not different from the state or liberal run groups and institutions. It seems that "conservative," "fundamental," Christians are scared to walk the path alone, being few in number, so they cower to those, who have abandoned the faith, believing we can associate ourselves with those who have abandoned the faith. What Would Jesus, Peter, Paul, James, or John say?

Acts 20:27-30 Updated American Standard Version (UASV)

27 for I did not shrink from declaring to you the whole purpose of God. **28** Pay careful attention to yourselves and to all the flock, in which the Holy Spirit has made you overseers, to care for the congregation[40] of God, which he obtained with the blood of his own Son.[41] **29** I know that **after my departure fierce wolves will come in among you**, not sparing the flock; **30** and **from among your own selves** men will arise, **speaking twisted things**, to **draw away <u>the disciples</u> after them**.

The opposition to the Truth and the Way did not come without numerous warnings from Jesus and the New Testament writers. Beginning with Jesus, the warning went out.

"[Jesus] Be Aware of False Prophets . . .

[Peter] There Will Be False Teachers Among You"

Jesus was well aware that the easiest way to defeat any group is to divide them, and so was Satan, who had been watching humanity for over 4,000 years, and especially the Israelites (Isaac and Ishmael / Jacob and Esau / Israel and Judah), as "Satan disguises himself as an angel of light. So it is no surprise if his servants, also, disguise themselves as servants of righteousness." (2 Cor. 11:14-15)

Where would these false teachers come from? Paul clearly says, to the Ephesian elders, about 56 C.E., "**from among your own selves** will arise men speaking twisted things." (Ac 20:29-30) Yes, these ones, who stand off from the Truth and the Way, would not be seeking their own disciples, but rather they would be seeking, "to draw away the disciples after them." i.e., the disciples of Christ.

The apostle Peter also spoke of these things about 64 C.E., "there will be false teachers among you, who will secretly bring in

---

[40] Gr *ekklesia* ("assembly;" "congregation, i.e., of Christians")

[41] Lit *with the blood of his Own*.

destructive heresies . . . in their greed they will exploit you with false words.." (2 Pet. 2:1, 3) These ones abandon the faithful words, become false teachers, rising within the Christian congregation, sharing their corrupting influence, intending to hide, disguise, or mislead.

These dire warnings by Jesus and the New Testament Authors had their beginnings in the first century C.E. Yes, they began small, but burst forth on the scene in the second century.

"[Paul says it] Is Already at Work"

About 51 C.E., some 1-years after Jesus' death, resurrection and ascension, division was already starting to creep into the faith, "the mystery of lawlessness is already at work." (2 Thess. 2:7) Yes, the power of the **lawlessness** was already present, which is the power of Satan, the god of this world (2 Cor. 4:4), and his tens of millions of demons, are hard at work behind the scenes.

There was even some divisions beginning as early as 49 C.E., when the elders wrote a letter to the Gentile believers, saying, "Since we have heard that some persons have gone out from us and troubled you with words, unsettling your minds, although we gave them no instructions" (Ac 15:24) Here we see that some *within*, were being very vocal about their opposition to the direction the faith was heading. Here, it was over whether the Gentiles needed to be circumcised, so as to be obedient to the Mosaic Law. (Ac 15:1, 5)

As the years progressed throughout the first-century, this divisive "talk ... spread like gangrene." (2 Tim. 2:17, c 65 C.E.) About 51 C.E., They had some in Thessalonica, at worst, going ahead of, or at best, misunderstanding Paul, and wrongly stating by word and a bogus letter "that the day of the Lord has come." (2 Thess. 2:1-2) In Corinth, about 55 C.E., "some of [were saying] that there is no resurrection of the dead. (1 Cor. 15:12) About 65 C.E., some were "saying that the resurrection has already happened. They [were] upsetting the faith of some." (2 Tim 2:16-18)

Throughout the next three decades, no inspired books were written. However, by the time of the apostle John's letter writing days of 96-98 C.E., he tells us, "now many antichrists have come. Therefore we know that it is the last hour." (1 John 2:18) These are ones, "who denies that Jesus is the Christ" and ones who not confess "Jesus Christ has come in the flesh is from God." (1 John 2:22; 4:2-3)

From 33 C.E. to 100 C.E., the apostles served Christ as a restraint against the great apostasy that was coming. Paul stated at 2 Thessalonians 2:7, "For the mystery of lawlessness is already at work. Only he [Apostle by Christ] who now restrains it [the great apostasy] will do so until he **[apostles]** is out of the way." 2 Thessalonians 2:3 said, "Let no one deceive you in any way **[misinterpretation or false teachers of Paul's first letter]**. For that day **[presence (second coming) of Christ]** will not come, unless the rebellion **[apostasy]** comes first, and the man of lawlessness **[likely one person, or maybe an organization / movement, empowered by Satan]** is revealed, the son of destruction"

We must keep in mind that the meaning of any given text is what the author meant by the words that he used, as should have been understood by his audience, and had some relevance/meaning for his audience. The rebellion [apostasy] began slowly in the first century, and would break forth after the death of the last apostle. Historians Will and Ariel Durant state, "Celsus [second-century enemy of Christianity] himself had sarcastically observed that Christians were 'split up into ever so many factions, each individual desiring to have his own party.' About 187 [C.E.] Irenaeus listed twenty varieties of Christianity; about 384 [C.E.] Epiphanius counted eighty." (*The Story of Civilization: Part III—Caesar and Christ*) Today we have 41,000 varieties of Christianity. What does it mean for the Christian, who has not abandoned inerrancy of Scripture, when someone abandons full or total inerrancy of Scripture? Let us listen to the words of Dr. Wayne Grudem,

Some theologians have argued that since human language is always in some sense "imperfect," any message that God addresses to us in human language must also be limited in its authority or truthfulness. But these passages and many others that record instances of God's words of personal address to individuals give no indication of any limitation of the authority or truthfulness of God's words when they are spoken in human language. Quite the contrary is true, for the words always place an absolute obligation upon the hearers to believe them and to obey them fully. **To disbelieve or disobey any part of them is to disbelieve or disobey God himself.** (Bold mine) Grudem, Wayne (2011). Making Sense of the Bible: One of Seven Parts from Grudem's Systematic Theology (Making Sense of Series) (p. 35). Zondervan.

Inerrancy of Scripture has to be the foundational doctrine, like no other. Why? If you remove it, you have no other. If inerrancy of Scripture is true, and it is, and one was teaching that it is not, what does that make them? If you willfully teach something that is not true, but rather is false, even though you believe it to be true, does that not make you a false teacher? A prophet of God is also and primarily so, a proclaimer of God's Word, namely, a teacher. What happens to false prophets and false teachers? God will deal with them his way, at Jesus' return, but for now, they are to be expelled from the church. What did John say, as to how we were to treat these ones? Did he say that we were to socialize with them, but just disagree with them doctrinally?

2 John 1:9-11 Updated American Standard Version (UASV)

⁹ Everyone who goes on ahead and does not remain in the teaching of Christ, does not have God; the one who remains in the teaching, he has both the Father and the Son. ¹⁰ If anyone comes to you and does not bring this teaching, do not receive him into your house or give him any greeting; ¹¹ for the one who gives him a greeting shares in his evil deeds.

"The teaching of Christ may refer to the teachings of Jesus or to teachings about Jesus. In either case, it refers to orthodox truth established and accepted in the church." The Holman New Testament Commentary by David Walls and Max Anders (p. 240) Yes, false teachers introduce their corrupt thinking into the church, and so should be removed to preserve the spirit of the church. Once removed, if unrepentant, what does John say our attitude toward them should be? We all have heard the phrase, 'guilt by association,' which means that when we socialize beyond being cordial; we are just as guilty as they are in the eyes of God. If a man wearing a clean white glove shakes the hand of a man wearing a soil-covered glove, does the clean clove make the dirty glove cleaner? On the other hand, does the grimy glove, make the clean glove dirtier?

These verses [1 John 1:9-11] seem harsh. Those who remain faithful to the teaching of Christ must resist those who do not. If a person did not teach truth about Jesus, these believers were not to practice hospitality toward him. This does not suggest that we are not to be cordial to false teachers, or that we cannot invite a member of a false sect into our home to talk with him. Rather, it refers to a level of hospitality that helps the false teacher spread his or her false doctrine.

In the first century, traveling was difficult. The traveler could not find hotels and restaurants. Traveling teachers and missionaries depended on others to house and feed them. John urged his readers not to "fund" these false teachers by housing and feeding them. To do so would be to share **in his wicked work.** In our day, when people of all sorts of religious belief use the media to plead for financial support, we need to be careful what kind of doctrine we fund. (IBID, 241)

The irony here is when authors like David Walls and Max Anders pen their commentaries, they are likely thinking of Jehovah's Witnesses, Mormons, and others as being the false teachers, by means of referring to them as a "false sect." Really? Is the rejection of the Trinity by the Jehovah's Witnesses any worse than the so-called Christian (Baptist, Presbyterian, etc.), who rejects the very Word of God that expounds on that doctrine and every other doctrine that is held dear? When someone is an unrepentant false teacher, they are to be removed from the church, and are not to be invited to social gatherings, nor are they to be spoken of in flattering terms within spoken or written words. If they repent, turn around, and change their ways, then time must pass, to see if this is really the case. Anyone standing off from the truth is an apostate of the church, an enemy of the church.

Review Questions

- What are the different levels of inerrancy?

- The Bible is what for many people today?

- How have many great Bible scholars entered the slippery slope of rejecting full or absolute inerrancy?

- What warning did the apostle Paul give to the Ephesian elders?

- Why can we say that no one who goes on ahead and does not remain in the teaching of Christ has God?

CHAPTER 4 Canonicity of the Bible

Canon of the New Testament

By J. S. Riggs

I. Two Preliminary Considerations.

The canon is the collection of 27 books which the church (generally) receives as its New Testament Scriptures. The history of the canon is the history of the process by which these books were brought together and their value as sacred Scriptures officially recognized. That process was gradual, furthered by definite needs, and, though unquestionably continuous, is in its earlier stages difficult to trace. It is always well in turning to the study of it to have in mind two considerations which bear upon the earliest phases of the whole movement. These are:

1. Early Christians Had the Old Testament:

The early Christians had in their hands what was a Bible to them, namely, the Old Testament Scriptures. These were used to a surprising extent in Christian instruction. For a whole century after the death of Jesus this was the case. These Scriptures were read in the churches, and there could be at first no idea of placing beside them new books which could for a moment rank with them in honor and authority. It has been once and again discussed whether Christianity from the first was a "book-religion." The decision of the matter depends upon what is referred to by the word "book." Christianity certainly did have from the very beginning a book which it reverenced--the Old Testament--but years passed before it had even the beginnings of a book of its own. What has been called "the wealth of living canonical material," namely, prophets and teachers, made written words of subordinate value. In this very teaching, however, with its oral traditions lay the beginnings of that movement which was ultimately to issue in a canon of writings.

2. No Intention of Writing the New Testament:

When the actual work of writing began no one who sent forth an epistle or framed a gospel had before him the definite purpose of contributing toward the formation of what we call "the Bible." All the New Testament writers looked for "the end" as

82

near. Their words, therefore, were to meet definite needs in the lives of those with whom they were associated. They had no thought of creating a new sacred literature. And yet these incidental occasional writings have come to be our choicest Scripture. The circumstances and influences which brought about this result are here briefly set forth.

II. Three Stages of the Process.

For convenience of arrangement and definiteness of impression the whole process may be marked off in three stages: (1) that from the time of the apostles until about 170 AD; (2) that of the closing years of the 2nd century and the opening of the 3rd (170-220 AD); (3) that of the 3rd and 4th centuries. In the first we seek for the evidences of the growth in appreciation of the peculiar value of the New Testament writings; in the second we discover the clear, full recognition of a large part of these writings as sacred and authoritative; in the third the acceptance of the complete canon in the East and in the West.

1. From the Apostles to 170 AD:

(1) Clement of Rome; Ignarius; Polycarp:

The first period extending to 170 AD.--It does not lie within the scope of this article to recount the origin of the several books of the New Testament. This belongs properly to New Testament Introduction (which see). By the end of the 1st century all of the books of the New Testament were in existence. They were, as treasures of given churches, widely separated and honored as containing the word of Jesus or the teaching of the apostles. From the very first the authority of Jesus had full recognition in all the Christian world. The whole work of the apostles was in interpreting Him to the growing church. His sayings and His life were in part for the illumination of the Old Testament; wholly for the understanding of life and its issues. In every assembly of Christians from the earliest days He was taught as well as the Old Testament. In each church to which an epistle was written that epistle was likewise read. Paul asked that his letters be read in this way (1 Thess. 5:27; Col 4:16). In this attentive listening to the exposition of some event in the life of Jesus or to the reading of the epistle of an apostle began the "authorization" of the traditions concerning Jesus and the apostolic writings. The widening of the area of the church and the departure of the apostles from earth emphasized increasingly the value of that which the writers of the New Testament left behind them. Quite early the desire to have the benefit of all possible instruction led to the interchange of Christian writings. Polycarp (110 AD ?) writes to the Philippians, "I have received letters from you and from Ignatius. You recommend me to send on yours to Syria; I shall do so either personally or by some other means. In return I send you the letter of Ignatius as well as others which I have in my hands and for which you made request. I add them to the present one; they will serve to edify your faith and perseverance" (Epistle to Phil, XIII). This is an illustration of what must have happened toward furthering a knowledge of the writings of the apostles. Just when and to what extent "collections" of our New Testament books began to be made it is impossible to say, but it is fair to infer that a collection of the Pauline epistles existed at the time Polycarp wrote to the Phil and when Ignatius wrote his seven letters to the churches of Asia Minor, i.e. about 115 AD. There is good reason to think also that the four Gospels were brought together in some places as early as this. A clear distinction, however, is to be kept in mind between "collections" and such recognition as we imply in the word "canonical." The gathering of books was one of the steps preliminary to this. Examination of the testimony to the New Testament in this early time indicates also that it is given with no intention of framing the canonicity of New Testament books. In numerous instances only "echoes" of the thought of the epistles appear; again quotations are incomplete; both showing that Scripture words are used as the natural expression of Christian thought. In the same way, the Apostolic Fathers refer to the teachings and deeds of Jesus. They witness "to the substance and not to the authenticity of the Gospels." That this all may be more evident let us note in more detail the witness of the subapostolic age.

Clement of Rome, in 95 AD, wrote a letter in the name of the Christians of Rome to those in Corinth. In this letter he uses material found in Mt, Lk, giving it a free rendering (see chapters 46 and 13); he has been much influenced by the Epistle to the Hebrews (see chapters 9, 10, 17, 19, 36). He knows Romans, Corinthians, and there are found echoes of 1 Timothy, Titus, 1 Peter and Ephesians.

The Epistles of Ignatius (115 AD) have correspondences with our gospels in several places (Eph 5:1-33; Ro 6:1-23; 7:1-25) and incorporate language from nearly all of the Pauline epistles. The Epistle to Polycarp makes large use of Phil, and besides this cites nine of the other Pauline epistles. Ignatius quotes from Matthew, apparently from memory; also from 1 Peter and 1 John. In regard to all these three writers--Clement, Polycarp, Ignatius--it is not enough to say that they bring us reminiscences or quotations from this or that book. Their thought is tinctured all through with New Testament truth. As we move a little farther down the years we come to "The Teaching of the Twelve Apostles" (circa 120 AD in its present form); the Epistle of Barnabas (circa 130 AD) and the Shepherd of Hermas (circa 130 AD). These exhibit the same phenomena as appear in the writings of Clement, Ignatius and Polycarp as far as references to the New Testament are concerned. Some books are quoted, and the thought of the three writings echoes again and again the teachings of the New Testament. They bear distinct witness to the value of "the gospel" and the doctrine of the apostles, so much so as to place these clearly above their own words. It is in the Epistle of Barnabas that we first come upon the phrase "it is written," referring to a New Testament book (Matthew) (see Epis., iv.14). In this deepening sense of value was enfolded the feeling of authoritativeness, which slowly was to find expression. It is well to add that what we have so far discovered was true in widely separated parts of the Christian world as e.g. Rome and Asia Minor.

(2) Forces Increasing Value of Writings:

(a) Apologists, Justin Martyr:

The literature of the period we are examining was not, however, wholly of the kind of which we have been speaking. Two forces were calling out other expressions of the singular value of the writings of the apostles, whether gospels or epistles. These were (a) the attention of the civil government in view of the rapid growth of the Christian church and (b) heresy. The first brought to the defense or commendation of Christianity the Apologists, among whom were Justin Martyr, Aristides, Melito of Sardis and Theophilus of Antioch. By far the most important of these was Justin Martyr, and his work may be taken as representative. He was born about 100 AD at Shechem, and died as a martyr at Rome in 165 AD. His two Apologies and the Dialogue with Trypho are the sources for the study of his testimony. He speaks of the "Memoirs of the Apostles called Gospels" (Ap., i.66) which were read on Sunday interchangeably with the prophets (i.67). Here emerges that equivalence in value of these "Gospels" with the Old Testament Scriptures which may really mark the beginning of canonization. That these Gospels were our four Gospels as we now have them is yet a disputed question; but the evidence is weighty that they were. (See Purves, Testimony of Justin Martyr to Early Christianity, Lect V.) The fact that Tatian, his pupil, made a harmony of the Gospels, i.e. of our four Gospels, also bears upon our interpretation of Justin's "Memoirs." (See Hemphill, The Diatessaron of Tatian.) The only other New Testament book which Justin mentions is the Apocalypse; but he appears to have known the Acts, six epistles of Paul, Hebrew and 1 John, and echoes of still other epistles are perceptible. When he speaks of the apostles it is after this fashion: "By the power of God they proclaimed to every race of men that they were sent by Christ to teach to all the Word of God" (Ap., i.39). It is debatable, however, whether this refers to more than the actual preaching of the apostles. The beginning of the formation of the canon is in the position and authority given to the Gospels.

(b) Gnostics, Marcion:

While the Apologists were busy commending or defending Christianity, heresy in the form of Gnosticism was also compelling attention to the matter of the writings of the apostles. From the beginning Gnostic teachers claimed that Jesus had favored chosen ones of His apostles with a body of esoteric truth which had been handed down by secret tradition. This the church denied, and in the controversy that went on through years the question of what were authoritative writings became more and more pronounced. Basilides e.g., who taught in Alexandria during the reign of Hadrian (AD 117-38), had for his secret authority the secret tradition of the apostle Matthias and of Glaucias, an alleged interpreter of Peter, but he bears witness to Matthew, Luke, John, Romans, 1 Corinthians, Ephesians, and Colossians in the effort to recommend his doctrines, and, what is more, gives them the value of Scripture in order to support more securely his teachings. (See Philosophoumena of Hippolytus,VII , 17). Valentinus, tracing his authority through Theodas to Paul, makes the same general use of New Testament books, and Tertullian tells us that he appeared to use the whole New Testament as then known.

The most noted of the Gnostics was Marcion, a native of Pontus. He went to Rome (circa 140 AD), there broke with the church and became a dangerous heretic. In support of his peculiar views, he formed a canon of his own which consisted of Luke's Gospel and ten of the Pauline epistles. He rejected the Pastoral Epistles, Hebrews, Matthew, Mark, John, the Acts, the Catholic epistles and the Apocalypse, and made a recension of both the gospel of Luke and the Pauline epistles which he accepted. His importance, for us, however, is in the fact that he gives us the first clear evidence of the canonization of the Pauline epistles. Such use of the Scriptures inevitably called forth both criticism and a clearer marking off of those books which were to be used in the churches opposed to heresy, and so "in the struggle with Gnosticism the canon was made." We are thus brought to the end of the first period in which we have marked the collection of New Testament books in greater or smaller compass, the increasing valuation of them as depositions of the truth of Jesus and His apostles, and finally the movement toward the claim of their authoritativeness as over against perverted teaching. No sharp line as to a given year can be drawn between the first stage of the process and the second. Forces working in the first go on into the second, but results are accomplished in the second which give it its right to separate consideration.

2. From 170 AD to 220 AD:

The period from 170 AD to 220 AD.--This is the age of a voluminous theological literature busy with the great issues of church canon and creed. It is the period of the great names of Irenaeus, Clement of Alexandria, and Tertullian, representing respectively Asia Minor, Egypt and North Africa. In passing into it we come into the clear light of Christian history. There is no longer any question as to a New Testament canon; the only difference of judgment is as to its extent. What has been slowly but surely shaping itself in the consciousness of the church now comes to clear expression.

(1) Irenaeus.

That expression we may study in Irenaeus as representative of the period. He was born in Asia Minor, lived and taught in Rome and became afterward bishop of Lyons. He had, therefore, a wide acquaintance with the churches, and was peculiarly competent to speak concerning the general judgment of the Christian world. As a pupil of Polycarp, who was a disciple of John, he is connected with the apostles themselves. An earnest defender of the truth, he makes the New Testament in great part his authority, and often appeals to it. The four Gospels, the Acts, the epistles of Paul, several of the Catholic epistles and the Apocalypse are to him Scripture in the fullest sense. They are genuine and authoritative, as much so as the Old Testament ever was. He dwells upon the fact that there are four gospels, the very number being prefigured in the four winds and the four quarters of the earth. Every attempt to increase or diminish the number is heresy. Tertullian takes virtually the same position (Adv. Marc., iv. 2), while Clement of Alexandria quotes all four gospels as "Scripture." By the end of the 2nd century the canon of the gospels was settled. The same is true also of the Pauline epistles. Irenaeus makes more than two hundred citations from Paul, and looks upon his epistles as Scripture (Adv. Haer., iii.12, 12). Indeed, at this time it may be said that the new canon was known under the designation "The Gospel and the Apostles" in contradistinction to the old as "the Law and the Prophets." The title "New Testament" appears to have been first used by an unknown writer against Montanism (circa 193 AD). It occurs frequently after this in Origen and later writers. In considering all this testimony two facts should have emphasis: (1) its wide extent: Clement and Irenaeus represent parts of Christendom which are widely separated; (2) the relation of these men to those who have gone before them. Their lives together with those before them spanned nearly the whole time from the apostles. They but voiced the judgment which silently, gradually had been selecting the "Scripture" which they freely and fully acknowledged and to which they made appeal.

(2) The Muratorian Fragment.

Just here we come upon the Muratorian Fragment, so called because discovered in 1740 by the librarian of Milan, Muratori. It dates from some time near the end of the 2nd century, is of vital interest in the study of the history of the canon, since it gives us a list of New Testament books and is concerned with the question of the canon itself. The document comes from Rome, and Lightfoot assigns it to Hippolytus. Its list contains the Gospels (the first line of the fragment is incomplete, beginning with Mark, but Matthew is clearly implied), the Acts, the Pauline epistles, the Apocalypse, 1 and 2 John (perhaps by implication the third) and Jude. It does not mention Hebrew, 1 and 2 Peter, James. In this list we have virtually the real position of the canon at the close of the 2nd century. Complete unanimity had not been attained in reference to all the books which are now between the covers of our New Testament. Seven books had not yet found a secure place beside the gospel and Paul in all parts of the church. The Palestinian and Syrian churches for a long time rejected the Apocalypse, while some of the Catholic epistles were in Egypt considered doubtful. The history of the final acceptance of these belongs to the third period.

3. 3rd and 4th Centuries:

(1) Origen:

The period included by the 3rd and 4th centuries--It has been said that "the question of the canon did not make much progress in the course of the 3rd century" (Reuss, History of the Canon of Holy Scripture, 125). We have the testimony of a few notable teachers mostly from one center, Alexandria. Their consideration of the question of the disputed book serves just here one purpose. By far the most distinguished name of the 3rd century is Origen. He was born in Alexandria about 185 AD, and before he was seventeen became an instructor in the school for catechumens. In 203 he was appointed bishop, experienced various fortunes, and died in 254. His fame rests upon his ability as an exegete, though he worked laboriously and successfully in other fields. His testimony is of high value, not simply because of his own studies, but also because of his wide knowledge of what was thought in other Christian centers in the world of his time. Space permits us only to give in summary form his conclusions, especially in regard to the books still in doubt. The Gospels, the Pauline epistles, the Acts, he accepts without question. He discusses at some length the authorship of He, believes that "God alone knows who wrote it," and accepts it as Scripture. His testimony to the Apocalypse is given in the sentence, "Therefore

John the son of Zebedee says in the Revelation." He also gives sure witness to Jude, but wavers in regard to James, 2 Peter, 2 John, and 3 John.

(2) Dionysius:

Another noted name of this century is Dionysius of Alexandria, a pupil of Origen (died 265). His most interesting discussion is regarding the Apocalypse, which he attributes to an unknown John, but he does not dispute its inspiration. It is a singular fact that the western church accepted this book from the first, while its position in the East was variable. Conversely the Epistle to the He was more insecure in the West than in the East. In regard to the Catholic epistles Dionysius supports James, 2 John, and 3 John, but not 2 Peter or Jude.

(3) Cyprian:

In the West the name of Cyprian, bishop of Carthage (248-58 AD), was most influential. He was much engaged in controversy, but a man of great personal force. The Apocalypse he highly honored, but he was silent about the Epistle to the Hebrews. He refers to only two of the Catholic epistles, 1 Peter and 1 John.

These testimonies confirm what was said above, namely, that the end of the 3rd century leaves the question of the full canon about where it was at the beginning. 1 Peter and 1 John seem to have been everywhere known and accepted. In the West the five Catholic epistles gained recognition more slowly than in the East.

(4) Eusebius:

In the early part of the 4th century Eusebius (270-340 AD), bishop of Caesarea before 315, sets before us in his Church History (III, chapters iii-xxv) his estimate of the canon in his time. He does not of course use the word canon, but he "conducts an historical inquiry into the belief and practice of earlier generations." He lived through the last great persecution in the early part of the 4th century, when not only places of worship were razed to the ground, but also the sacred Scriptures were in the public market-places consigned to the flames (Historia Ecclesiastica, VIII, 2). It was, therefore, no idle question what book a loyal Christian must stand for as his Scripture. The question of the canon had an earnest, practical significance. Despite some obscurity and apparent contradictions, his classification of the New Testament books was as follows: (1) The acknowledged books. His criteria for each of these was authenticity and apostolicity and he placed in this list the Gospels, Acts, and Paul's epistles, including He. (2) The disputed books, i.e. those which had obtained only partial recognition, to which he assigned Jas, Jude, 2 Pet and 2 Jn. About the Apocalypse also he was not sure. In this testimony there is not much advance over that of the 3rd century. It is virtually the canon of Origen. All this makes evident the fact that as yet no official decision nor uniformity of usage in the church gave a completed canon. The time, however, was drawing on when various forces at work were to bring much nearer this unanimity and enlarge the list of acknowledged books. In the second half of the 4th century repeated efforts were made to put an end to uncertainty.

(5) Athanasius:

Athanasius in one of his pastoral letters in connection with the publishing of the ecclesiastical calendar gives a list of the books comprising Scripture, and in the New Testament portion are included all the 27 books which we now recognize. "These are the wells of salvation," he writes, "so that he who thirsts may be satisfied with the sayings in these. Let no one add to these. Let nothing be taken away." Gregory of Nazianzen (died 390 AD) also published a list omitting Revelation, as did Cyril of Jerusalem (died 386), and quite at the end of the century (4th) Isidore of Pelusium speaks of the "canon of truth, the Divine Scriptures." For a considerable time the Apocalypse was not accepted in the Palestinian or Syrian churches. Athanasius helped toward its acceptance in the church of Alexandria. Some differences of opinion, however, continued. The Syrian church did not accept all of the Catholic epistles until much later.

(6) Council of Carthage, Jerome; Augustine:

The Council of Carthage in 397, in connection with its decree "that aside from the canonical Scriptures nothing is to be read in church under the name of Divine Scriptures," gives a list of the books of the New Testament. After this fashion there was an endeavor to secure unanimity, while at the same time differences of judgment and practice continued. The books which had varied treatment through these early centuries were He, the Apocalypse and the five minor Catholic epistles. The advance of Christianity under Constantine had much to do with the reception of the whole group of books in the East. The task which the emperor gave to Eusebius to prepare "fifty copies of the Divine Scriptures" established a standard which in time gave recognition to all doubtful books. In the West, Jerome and Augustine were the controlling factors in its settlement of the canon. The publication of the Vulgate (Jerome's Latin Bible, 390-405 A.D.) virtually determined the matter.

In conclusion let it be noted how much the human element was involved in the whole process of forming our New Testament. No one would wish to dispute a providential overruling of it all. Also it is well to bear in mind that all the books have not the same clear title to their places in the canon as far as the history of their attestation is concerned. Clear and full and unanimous, however, has been the judgment from the beginning upon the Gospels, the Acts, the Pauline epistles, 1 Peter and 1 John.

Canon of the Old Testament

By George L. Robinson

I. Introductory.

The problem of how we came by 39 books known as Old Testament "Scripture" is a purely historical investigation. The question involved is, not who wrote the several books, but who made them into a collection, not their origin or contents, but their history; not God's part, but man's. Our present aim, accordingly, must be to trace the process by which the various writings became "Scripture."

1. The Christian Term "Canon":

The word "canon" is of Christian origin, from the Greek word kanon, which in turn is probably borrowed from the Hebrew word, qaneh, meaning a reed or measuring rod, hence, norm or rule. Later it came to mean a rule of faith, and eventually a catalogue or list. In present usage it signifies a collection of religious writings Divinely inspired and hence, authoritative, normative, sacred and binding. The term occurs in Ga 6:16; 2Co 10:13-16; but it is first employed of the books of Scripture in the technical sense of a standard collection or body of sacred writings, by the church Fathers of the 2Co 4:1-18th century; e.g. in the 59th canon of the Council of Laodicea (363 AD); in the Festal Epistle of Athanasius (365 AD); and by Amphilochius, archbishop of Iconium (395 AD).

2. The Corresponding Hebrew Expression:

How the ancient Hebrews expressed the conception of canonicity is not known; but it is safe to say that the idea, as an idea, existed long before there was any special phrase invented to express it. In the New Testament the word "Scriptures" conveys unquestionably the notion of sacredness (Mt 21:42; Joh 5:39; Ac 18:24). From the 1st century AD and following, however, according to the Talmud, the Jews employed the phrase "defile the hands." Writings which were suitable to be read in the synagogue were designated as books which "defile the hands." What this very peculiar oriental expression may have originally signified no one definitely knows. Probably Le 16:24 gives a hint of the true interpretation. According to this passage the high priest on the great Day of Atonement washed not only when he put on the holy garments of his office, but also when he put them off. Quite possibly, therefore, the expression "defile the hands" signified that the hands which had touched the sacred writings must first be washed before touching aught else. The idea expressed, accordingly, was one akin to that of taboo. That is to say, just as certain garments worn by worshippers in encircling the sacred Kaaba at Mecca are taboo to the Mohammedans of today, i.e. cannot be worn outside the mosque, but must be left at the door as the worshippers quit the sanctuary, so the Hebrew writings which were fit to be read in the synagogue rendered the hands of those who touched them taboo, defiling their hands, as they were wont to say, so that they must first be washed before engaging in any secular business. This seems to be the best explanation of this enigmatical phrase. Various other and somewhat fanciful explanations of it, however, have been given: for example, to prevent profane uses of worn-out synagogue rolls (Buhl); or to prevent placing consecrated grain alongside of the sacred rolls in the synagogues that it might become holy, as the grain would attract the mice and the mice would gnaw the rolls

(Strack, Wildeboer and others); or to prevent the sacred, worn-out parchments from being used as coverings for animals (Graetz); or to "declare the hands to be unclean unless previously washed" (Furst, Green). But no one of these explanations satisfies. The idea of taboo is more likely imbedded in the phrase.

3. The "Hidden Books" of the Jews:

The rabbins invented a special phrase to designate rolls that were worn- out or disputed. These they called genuzim, meaning "hidden away." Cemeteries filled with Hebrew manuscripts which have long been buried are frequently found today in Egypt in connection with Jewish synagogues. Such rolls might first be placed in the genizah or rubbish chamber of the sanctuary. They were not, however, apocryphal or uncanonical in the sense of being extraneous or outside the regular collection. For such the Jews had a special term cepharim chitsonim, "books that are outside." These could not be read in the synagogues. "Hidden books" were rather worn-out parchments, or canonical rolls which might by some be temporarily disputed.

4. The Determining Principle in the Formation of the Canon:

Who had the right to declare a writing canonical? To this question widely divergent answers have been given. According to a certain class of theologians the several books of the Old Testament were composed by authors who were conscious not only of their inspiration but also that their writings were destined to be handed down to the church of future generations as sacred. In other words each writer canonized, as it were, his own writings. For example, Dr. W. H. Green (Canon, 35 f, 106, 110) says: "No formal declaration of their canonicity was needed to give them sanction. They were from the first not only eagerly read by the devout but believed to be Divinely obligatory .... Each individual book of an acknowledged prophet of Yahweh, or of anyone accredited as inspired by Him to make known His will, was accepted as the word of God immediately upon its appearance. .... Those books and those only were accepted as the Divine standards of their faith and regulative of their conduct which were written for this definite purpose by those whom they believed to be inspired of God. It was this which made them canonical. The spiritual profit found in them corresponded with and confirmed the belief in their heavenly origin. And the public official action which further attested, though it did not initiate, their canonicity, followed in the wake of the popular recognition of their Divine authority. .... The writings of the prophets, delivered to the people as a declaration of the Divine will, possessed canonical authority from the moment of their appearance. .... The canon does not derive its authority from the church, whether Jewish or Christian; the office of the church is merely that of a custodian and a witness." So likewise Dr. J. D. Davis (Pres. and Ref. Review, April, 1902, 182).

On the contrary, Dillmann (Jahrb. fur deutsche Theol., III, 420) more scientifically claims that "history knows nothing of the individual books having been designed to be sacred from their origin. .... These books bore indeed in themselves from the first those characteristics on account of which they were subsequently admitted into the sacred collection, but yet always had first to pass through a shorter or longer period of verification, and make trial of the Divine power resident within them upon the hearts of the church before they were outwardly and formally acknowledged by it as Divine books." As a matter of fact, the books of the Old Testament are still on trial, and ever will be. So far as is known, the great majority of the writers of Holy Scripture did not arbitrarily hand over their productions to the church and expect them to be regarded as canon Scripture. Two parties are involved in the making of canonical Scripture--the original authors and the church--both of whom were inspired by the same Spirit. The authors wrote inspired by the Divine Spirit, and the church ever since--Jewish and Christian alike--has been inspired to recognize the authoritative character of their writings. And so it will be to the end of time. "We cannot be certain that anything comes from God unless it bring us personally something evidently Divine" (Briggs, The Study of Holy Scripture, 162).

5. The Tripartite Division of the Old Testament:

The Jews early divided the Old Testament writings into three classes: (1) the Torah, or Law; (2) the Nebhi'im, or Prophets; and (3) the Kethubhim, or Writings, called in Greek the Hagiographa. The Torah included the 5 books of the Pentateuch (Genesis, Exodus, Leviticus, Numbers, Deuteronomy), which were called "the Five-fifths of the Law." The Nebhi'im embraced (a) the four so-called Former Prophets, Joshua, Judges, 1 and 2 Samuel, counted as one book, 1 and 2 Kings, also counted as one book; and (b) the four so-called Latter Prophets, Isaiah, Jeremiah, Ezekiel, and the Twelve Minor Prophets, counted as one book; a total of 8 books. The Kethubhim, or Writings, were 11 in all, including Psalms, Proverbs, and Job, the five Meghilloth or Rolls (Canticles, Ruth, Lamentations, Ecclesiastes, Esther), Daniel, Ezra-Nehemiah, counted as one book, and 1 and 2 Chronicles, also counted as one book; in all 24 books, exactly the same as those of the Protestant canon. This was the original count of the Jews as far as we can trace it back. Later certain Jewish authorities appended Ruth to Judges, and Lamentations to Jer, and thereby obtained the number 22, which corresponded to the number of letters in the Hebrew alphabet; but this manner of counting was secondary and fanciful. Still later others divided Samuel, Kings, Chronicles, Ezra-Nehemiah and Jeremiah-Lamentations into two books each respectively and thereby obtained 27, which they fancifully regarded as equivalent to the 22 letters of the Hebrew alphabet plus 5, the number of letters having a peculiar final form when standing at the end of a word. Jerome states that 22 is the correct reckoning, but he adds, "Some count both Ruth and Lamentations among the Hagiographa, and so get 24." 4 Esdras, which is the oldest (85-96 AD) witness to the number of books in the Old Testament, gives 24.

6. How Account for the Tripartite Division?:

The answer to the question of how to account for the tripartite division involves the most careful investigation of the whole process by which the canon actually took shape. If the entire canon of the Old Testament were formed, as some allege, by one man, or by one set of men, in a single age, then it is obvious that the books must have been separated into three groups on the basis of some material differences in their contents. If, on the other hand; the process of canonization was gradual and extended over several generations, then the various books were separated from one another probably because one section of the canon was closed before certain other books of similar character were written. At any rate it is difficult to see why Kings and Chronicles are not included in the same division, and especially strange that Daniel does not stand among the prophets. To explain this mystery, medieval Jews were wont to say that "the Prophets were inspired by the spirit of prophecy, whereas the Writings by the Holy Spirit," implying different degrees of inspiration. But this is a distinction without a difference, the Holy Spirit and the spirit of prophecy are one and the same. Modern Protestants distinguish between the donum propheticum and the munus propheticum, i.e. between the gift and the office of prophecy. They allow that Daniel possessed the gift of prophecy, but they deny that he was Divinely appointed to the office of prophet. But compare Mt 24:15, which speaks of "Daniel the prophet," and on the other hand, Am 7:14, in which Amos resents being considered a prophet. Oehler modifies this explanation, claiming that the threefold division of the canon corresponds to the three stages of development in the religion of Israel, namely, Mosaism, Prophetism, and Hebraism. According to Oehler, the Law was the foundation of the entire canon. From it there were two lines of development, one objective, the Prophets, the other subjective, the Writings. But Oehler's theory does not satisfactorily account for Ezra and Nehemiah and Chronicles, being in the third division; for in what sense can they be said to be more subjective than Judges, Samuel, and Kings? The Septuagint version (250-150 BC) takes no notice of the tripartite division. The true solution probably is that the process was gradual. When all the witnesses have been examined, we shall probably discover that the Law was canonized first, the Prophets considerably later, and the Writings last of all. And it may further become evident that the two last divisions were collected synchronously, and hence, that the tripartite divisions of the canon are due to material differences in their contents as well as to chronology.

II. Examination of the Witnesses.

1. The Old Testament's Witness to Itself (circa 1450-444 BC):

Though the Old Testament does not tell us anything about the processes of its own canonization, it does furnish valuable hints as to how the ancient Hebrews preserved their writings. Thus in Ex 40:20 it is stated that the "testimony," by which is meant the two tables of the Law containing the Ten Commandments, was put into the Ark of the Covenant for safe-keeping. In De 31:9, 24-26, the laws of Deuteronomy are said to have been delivered to the sons of Levi, and by them deposited "by the side of the ark .... that it may be there for a witness against thee." Such language indicates that the new lawbook is regarded "as a standard of faith and action" (Driver, Deuteronomy, 343). According to 1Ki 8:9, when Solomon brought the Ark up from the city of David to the Temple, the two tables were still its only contents, which continued to be carefully preserved. According to 2Ki 11:12, when Joash was crowned king, Jehoiada the high priest is said to have given (literally "put upon") him "the testimony," which doubtless contained "the substance of the fundamental laws of the covenant," and was regarded as "the fundamental charter of the constitution" (compare H. E. Ryle, Canon of the Old Testament 45). Likewise in Pr 25:1, it is stated that a large number of proverbs were copied out by Hezekiah's men. Now all these, and still other passages which might be summoned, witness to the preservation of certain portions of the Old Testament. But preservation is not synonymous with canonization. A writing might easily be preserved without being made a standard of faith and conduct. Nevertheless the two ideas are closely related; for, when religious writings are sedulously preserved it is but natural to infer that their intrinsic value was regarded as correspondingly precious.

Two other passages of paramount importance remain to be considered. The first is 2Ki 22:8ff, describing the finding of the "Book of the Law," and how Josiah the king on the basis of it instituted a religious reformation and bound the people to obey it precepts. Here is an instance in which the Law, or some portion of it (how much no one can say), is regarded as of normative and authoritative character. The king and his coadjutators recognize at once that it is ancient and that it contains the words of Yahweh (2Ki 22:13, 18-19). Its authority is undisputed. Yet nothing is said of its "canonicity," or that it would "defile the hands"; consequently there is no real ground for speaking of it as "the beginnings of the canon," for in the same historic sense the beginnings of the canon are to be found in Ex 24:7. The other passage of paramount importance is Ne 8:8f, according to which Ezra is said to have "read in the book, in the law of God, distinctly." Not only did Ezra read the Law; he accompanied it with an interpretation. This seems to imply, almost beyond question, that in Ezra's time (444 BC) the Law, i.e. the Pentateuch, was regarded as canonical Scripture. This is practically all that the Old Testament says about itself, though other passages, such as Zec 7:12 and Da 9:2 might be brought forward to show the deep regard which the later prophets had for the writings of their predecessors. The former of these is the locus classicus in the Old Testament, teaching the inspiration of the Prophets; it is the Old Testament parallel to 2Ti 3:16.

2. The Samaritan Pentateuch (circa 432 BC):

Chronologically the Old Testament is of course our most ancient witness. It brings us down to 444 BC. The next in order is the Samaritan Pentateuch, the history of which is as follows: About 432 BC, as we know from Ne 13:28 and Josephus (Ant., XI, vii, 2 through viii, 4), Nehemiah expelled from the Jewish colony in Jerusalem Manasseh, the polygamous grandson of Eliashib the high priest and son-in-law of Sanballat. Manasseh founded the schismatic community of the Samaritans, and instituted on Mt. Gerizim a rival temple worship to that at Jerusalem. Of the Samaritans there still survive today some 170 souls; they reside in Shechem and are known as "the smallest religious sect in the world." It is true that Josephus, speaking of this event, confuses chronology somewhat, making Nehemiah and Alexander the Great contemporaries, whereas a century separated them, but the time element is of little moment. The bearing of the whole matter upon the history of the formation of the canon is this: the Samaritans possess the Pentateuch only; hence, it is inferred that at the time of Manasseh's expulsion the Jewish canon included the Pentateuch and the Pentateuch only. Budde (Encyclopaedia Biblica col. 659) says: "If alongside of the Law there had been other sacred writings, it would be inexplicable why these last also did not pass into currency with the Samaritans." Such a conclusion, however, is not fully warranted. It is an argument from silence. There are patent reasons on the other hand why the Samaritans should have rejected the Prophets, even though the y were already canonized. For the Samaritans would hardly adopt into their canon books that glorified the temple at Jerusalem. It cannot, accordingly, be inferred with certainty from the fact that the Samaritans accept the Pentateuch only, that therefore the Pentateuch at the time of Manasseh's expulsion was alone canonical, though it may be considered a reasonable presumption.

3. The Septuagint Version (circa 250-150 BC):

The Septuagint version in Greek is the first translation of the Old Testament ever made; indeed the Old Testament is the first book of any note in all literature to receive the honor of being translated into another tongue. This fact in itself is indicative of the esteem in which it was held at the time. The work of translation was inaugurated by Ptolemy Philadelphus (285-247 BC) and probably continued for well-nigh a century (circa 250-150 BC). Aristeas, a distinguished officer of Ptolemy, records how it came about. It appears that Ptolemy was exceedingly fond of books, and set his heart on adding to his famous collection in Alexandria a translation of the Hebrew Pentateuch In order to obtain it, so the story goes, the king set free 198,000 Jewish slaves, and sent them with presents to Jerusalem to ask Eleazar the high priest for their Law and Jewish scholars capable of translating it. Six learned rabbis from each tribe (6 X 12 = 72) were sent. They were royally feasted; 70 questions were asked them to test their wisdom, and after 72 days of cooperation and conference they gave the world the Old Testament in the Greek language, which is known as the Septuagint version. To this fabulous story, Christian tradition adds that the rabbis did the work of translating in 72 (some say 36) separate cells on the island of Pharos, all working independently of each other, and that it was found at the expiration of their seclusion that each had produced a translation exactly word for word alike, hence, supernaturally inspired. Justin Martyr of the 2nd century AD says that he was actually shown by his Alexandrian guide the ruins of these Septuagint cells. The story is obviously a fable. The kernel of real truth at the bottom of it is probably that Ptolemy Philadelphus about the middle of the 3rd century BC succeeded in obtaining a translation of the Law. The other books were translated subsequently, perhaps for private use. The lack of unity of plan in the books outside the Law indicates that probably many different hands at different times were engaged upon them. There is a subscription, moreover, at the close of the translation of Est which states that Lysimachus, the son of Ptolemy in Jerusalem, translated it. But the whole was apparently completed before Jesus ben Sirach the younger wrote his Prologue to Ecclesiasticus (circa 132 BC).

Now the Septuagint version, which was the Bible of our Lord and His apostles, is supposed to have included originally many of the Apocryphal books. Furthermore, in our present Septuagint, the canonical and Apocryphal books stand intermingled and in an order which shows that the translators knew nothing of the tripartite division of later Judaism, or if they did they quite ignored it. The order of the books in our English Old Testament is of course derived from the Septuagint through the Vulgate (Jerome's Latin Bible, 390-405 A.D.) of Jerome. The books in the Septuagint are arranged as follows: Pentateuch, Joshua, Judges, Ruth, 1 and 2 Samuel, 1 and 2 Kings, 1 and 2 Chronicles, 1 and 2 Esdras, Nehemiah, Tobit, Judith, Esther, Job, Psalms, Proverbs, Ecclesiastes, Wisdom, Ecclesiasticus, Hosea, Amos, Micah, Joel, Obadiah, Jonah, Nahum, Habakkuk, Zepheniah, Hagai, Zechariah, Malachi, Isaiah, Jeremiah, Baruch, Lamentations, Ep. Jer., Ezekiel, Daniel, 1, 2 and 3 Maccabees. On the basis of the Septuagint, Catholics advocate what is known as the "larger" canon of the Jews in Alexandria; Protestants, on the other hand, deny the existence of an independent canon in Alexandria in view of the "smaller" canon of the Jews in Palestine The actual difference between the Catholic and Protestant Old Testaments is a matter of 7 complete books and portions of two others: namely, Tobit, Judith, Wisdom, Ecclesiasticus, Baruch, 1 and 2 Maccabees, together with certain additions to Esther (Est 10:4 through 16:24) and to Daniel (Da 3:24-30; The Song of the Three Holy Children (Azariah); Susanna verse 13 and Bel and the Dragon verse 14). These Protestants reject as apocryphal because there is no sufficient evidence that they were ever reckoned as canonical by the Jews anywhere. The fact that the present Septuagint includes them is far from conclusive that the original Septuagint did, for the following reasons: (1) The design of the Septuagint was purely literary; Ptolemy and the Alexandrians were interested in building up a library. (2) All the extant manuscripts of the Septuagint are of Christian not Jewish origin. Between the actual translation of the Septuagint (circa 250-150 BC) and the oldest manuscripts of the Septuagint extant (circa 350 AD) there is a chasm of fully 500 years, during which it is highly possible that the so-called Apocryphal books crept in. (3) In the various extant manuscripts of the Septuagint, the Apocryphal books vary in number and name. For example, the great Vatican MS, which is probably "the truest representative which remains of the Alexandrian Bible," and which comes down to us from the 4th century AD, contains no Book of Maccabees whatever, but does include 1 Esdras, which Jerome and Catholics generally treat as apocryphal. On the other hand, the Alexandrian MS, another of the great manuscripts of the Septuagint, dating from the 5th century AD, contains not only the extra-canonical book of 1 Esdras, but 3 and 4 Maccabees, and in the New Testament the 1st and 2nd Epistles of Clement, none of which, however, is considered canonical by Rome. Likewise the great Sinaiticus MS, hardly less important than the Vatican as a witness to the Septuagint and like it dating from the 4th century AD, omits Baruch (which Catholics consider canonical), but includes 4 Macc, and in the New Testament the Epistle of Barnabas and the Shepherd of Hermas; all of which are excluded from the canon by Catholics. In other manuscripts, 3 Maccabees, 3 Esdras and The Prayer of Manasseh are occasionally included. The problem as to how many books the original Septuagint version actually included is a very complicated one. The probability is that it included no one of these variants. (4) Still another reason for thinking that there never existed in Egypt a separate or "larger" canon is the fact that during the 2nd century AD, the Alexandrian Jews adopted Aquila's Greek version of the Old Testament in lieu of their own, and it is known that Aquila's text excluded all Apocryphal books. Add to all this the fact that Philo, who lived in Alexandria from circa 20 BC till 50 AD, never quotes from One of these Apocryphal books though he often does from the canonical, and that Origen, who also resided in Alexandria (circa 200 AD), never set his imprimatur upon them, and it becomes reasonably convincing that there was no "larger" canon in Alexandria. The value of the evidence derived from the Septuagint, accordingly, is largely negative. It only indicates that when the translation of the Old Testament into Greek was made in Alexandria, the process of canonization was still incomplete. For had it been actually complete, it is reasonable to suppose that the work of translation would have proceeded according to some well-defined plan, and would have been executed with greater accuracy. As it is, the translators seem to have taken all sorts of liberties with the text, adding to the books of Est and Dan and omitting fully one-eighth of the text of Jer. Such work also indicates that they were not executing a public or ecclesiastical trust, but rather a private enterprise. Our necessary conclusion, therefore, is that the work of canonization was probably going on in Palestine while the work of translation was proceeding in Alexandria.

4. Ecclesiasticus, or the Wisdom of Jesus ben Sirach (circa 170 BC):

Our next witness is Jesus ben Sirach who (circa 170 BC) wrote a formidable work entitled Ecclesiasticus, otherwise known as Sir. The author lived in Jerusalem and wrote in Hebrew. His book is a book of Wisdom resembling Proverbs; some of his precepts approach the high level of the Gospel. In many respects Ecclesiasticus is the most important of all the Apocryphal books; theologically it is the chief monument of primitive Sadduceeism. In chapters 44 through 50, the author sings a "hymn to the Fathers," eulogizing the mighty heroes of Israel from Enoch to Nehemiah, in fact from Adam to Simon, including the most famous men described in the Old Testament, and making explicit mention of the Twelve Prophets. These facts would indicate that the whole or, at least, the most of the Old Testament was known to him, and that already in his day (180 BC) the so-called Minor Prophets were regarded as a special group of writings by themselves. What the value of Ecclesiasticus is as a witness, however, depends upon the interpretation one places on 24:33, which reads: "I will yet pour out doctrine as prophecy and leave it unto generations of ages." From this it is inferred by some that he feels himself inspired and capable of adding to the canon already in existence, and that, though he knew the full prophetic canon, he did not draw any very definite line of demarcation between his own work and the inspired writings of the prophets. For example, he passes over from the patriarchs and prophets of Israel to Simon the son of Onias, who was probably the high priest in his own time, making no distinction between them. But this may have been partly due to personal conceit; compare 39:12, "Yet more willI utter, whichI have thought upon; andI am filled as the moon at the full." Yet, perhaps, in his day still only the Law and the Prophets were actually canonized, but alongside of these a body of literature was being gathered and gradually augmented of a nature not foreign to his own writings, and therefore not clearly marked off from literary compositions like his own. Yet to Sirach the Law is everything. He identifies it with the highest Wisdom; indeed, all wisdom in his judgment is derived from a study of the Law (compare Sirach 19:20-24; 15:1-18; 24:23; 2:16; 39:1).

5. The Prologue to Ecclesiasticus (circa 132 BC):

The Prologue or Preface to Ecclesiasticus is our next witness to the formation of the canon. It was written by the grandson of Jesus ben Sirach, who bore his grandfather's name (circa 132 BC). Jesus ben Sirach the younger translated in Egypt his grandfather's proverbs into Greek, and in doing so added a Preface or Prologue of his own. In this Prologue, he thrice refers to the tripartite division of the Old Testament. In fact the Prologue to Ecclesiasticus is the oldest witness we have to the threefold division of the Old Testament books. He says: "Whereas many and great things have been delivered unto us by the Law and the Prophets, and by others, ... my grandfather, Jesus, when he had given himself to the reading of the Law, and the Prophets, and other books of our Fathers, and had gotten therein good judgment (the Revised Version (British and American) "having gained great familiarity therein"), was drawn on also himself to write something pertaining to learning and wisdom. .... For the same things uttered in Hebrew and translated into another tongue, have not the same force in them; and not only these things, but the Law itself, and the Prophets, and the rest of the books, have no small difference, when they are spoken in their own language." These are explicit and definite allusions to the threefold division of the Old Testament writings, yet only the titles of the first and second divisions are the technical names usually employed; the third is especially vague because of his use of the terms, "the other books of the Fathers," and "the rest of the books." However, he evidently refers to writings with religious contents; and, by "the other books of the Fathers," he can hardly be supposed to have meant an indefinite number, though he has not told us which they were or what was their number. From his further statement that his grandfather, having immersed himself in the Law and the Prophets, and other books of the Fathers, felt drawn on also himself to write something for the profit of others, it may be inferred that in his time there was as yet no definite gulf fixed between canonical writings and those of other men, and that the sifting process was still going on (compare W. R. Smith, OTJC2, 178-79).

6. 1 and 2 Maccabee (between 125 and 70 BC):

1 Maccabee was written originally in Hebrew; 2 Maccabee in Greek, somewhere between 125 and 70 BC. The author of 1 Maccabee is acquainted, on the one hand, with the deeds of John Hyrcanus (135 to 105 BC), and knows nothing on the other of the conquest of Palestine by Pompey (63 BC). The value of this book as a witness to the history of the canon centers about his allusions to Daniel and the Psalms. In 1 Macc 1:54, he tells how Antiochus Epiphanes "set up the abomination of desolation" upon the altar at Jerusalem, referring most likely to Da 9:24-27; and in 1 Macc 2:59,60 he speaks of Ananias, Azarias and Misael, who by believing were saved from the fiery furnace, and of Daniel, who was delivered from the mouths of the lions (compare Da 1:7; 3:26; 6:23). From these allusions, it would seem as though the Book of Daniel was at that time regarded as normative or canonical. This is confirmed by 1 Macc 7:16,17, which introduces a quotation from Ps 79:2, with the solemn formula, "According to the words which he wrote"; which would suggest that the Ps also were already canonical.

2 Maccabee, written circa 124 BC, also contains a couple of passages of considerable importance to us in this investigation. Both, however, are found in a spurious letter purporting to have been sent by the inhabitants of Judea to their fellow-countrymen residing in Egypt. The first passage (2 Macc 2:13) tells how Nehemiah, "founding a library, gathered together the acts of the kings, and the prophets, and of David, and the epistles of the kings concerning holy gifts." These words throw no special light upon the formation of the canon, but they do connect with the name of Nehemiah the preservation of public documents and historical records of national interest, and how he, as a lover of books, founded a library. This is in perfect agreement with what we know of Nehemiah's character, for he compiled the genealogy of Ne 7:1-73; besides, collection precedes selection. The other passage (2 Macc 2:14) reads: "In like manner also Judas gathered together all things that were lost by reason of the war we had, and they remain with us." Though found in a letter, supposed to be spurious, there is every reason for believing this statement to be true. For when Antiochus, the arch enemy of the nation, sought to stamp out the religion of the Jews by destroying their

books (compare 1 Macc 1:56,57), what would have been more natural for a true patriot like Judas than to attempt to re-collect their sacred writings? "This statement, therefore," as Wildeboer says, "may well be worthy of credence" (The Origin of the Canon of the Old Testament, 40). Though it yields nothing definite as to the number of the books recovered, it is obvious that the books collected were the most precious documents which the nation possessed. They were doubtless religious, as was the age.

7. Philo (circa 20 BC-50 AD):

Philo is our next witness. He flourished in Alexandria between circa 20 BC and 50 AD, leaving behind him a voluminous literature. Unfortunately, he does not yield us much of positive value for our present purpose. His evidence is largely negative. True, he nowhere mentions the tripartite division of the Old Testament, which is known to have existed in his day. Nor does he quote from Ezekiel, the Five Megilloth (Canticles, Ruth, Lamentations, Ecclesiastes, Esther), Daniel, Chronicles, or from the Twelve Minor Prophets, except Hosea, Jonah, and Zechariah. Moreover he held a loose view of inspiration. According to Philo, inspiration was by no means confined to the sacred Scriptures; all truly wise and virtuous men are inspired and capable of expressing the hidden things of God. But as Dr. Green (Canon, 130) right fully contends, "Philo's loose views of inspiration cannot be declared irreconcilable with the acceptance of a fixed canon, unless it is first shown that he places others whom he thinks inspired on a level with the writers of Scripture. This he never does." Philo's reverence for the "Law" was unbounded. In this respect he is the type of other Alexandrians. He quotes predominatingly from the Law. Moses was to him the source of all wisdom, even the wisdom of the Gentiles. Concerning the laws of Moses, he is reported by Eusebius as saying: "They have not changed so much as a single word in them. They would rather die a thousand deaths than detract anything from these laws and statutes." On the other hand, Philo never quotes any of the Apocryphal books. Hence, it may safely be assumed that his canon was essentially ours.

8. The New Testament as a Witness (circa 50-100 AD):

The evidence furnished by the New Testament is of the highest importance. When summed up, it gives the unmistakable impression that when the New Testament was written (circa 50-100 AD) there was a definite and fixed canon of Old Testament Scripture, to which authoritative appeal could be made. And first, too much importance can scarcely be attached to the names or titles ascribed to the Old Testament writings by the authors of the New Testament: thus, "the scripture" (Joh 10:35; 19:36; 2Pe 1:20), "the scriptures" (Mt 22:29; Ac 18:24), "holy scriptures" (Ro 1:2), "sacred writings" (2Ti 3:15), "the law" (Joh 10:34; 12:34; 15:25; 1Co 14:21), "law and prophets" (Mt 5:17; 7:12; 22:40; Lu 16:16; 24:44; Ac 13:15; 28:23). Such names or titles, though they do not define the limits of the canon, certainly assume the existence of a complete and sacred collection of Jewish writings which are already marked off from all other literature as separate and fixed. One passage (Joh 10:35) in which the term "scripture," is employed seems to refer to the Old Testament canon as a whole; "and the scripture cannot be broken." In like manner the expression "law and prophets" is often used in a generic sense, referring to much more than merely the 1st and 2nd divisions of the Old Testament; it seems rather to refer to the old dispensation as a whole; but the term "the law" is the most general of all. It is frequently applied to the entire Old Testament, and apparently held in Christ's time among the Jews a place akin to that which the term "the Bible" does with us. For example, in Joh 10:34; 11:34; 15:25, texts from the prophets or even from the Ps are quoted as part of "the Law"; in 1Co 14:21 also, Paul speaks of Isa 28:11 as a part of "the law." These names and titles, accordingly, are exceedingly important; they are never applied by New Testament writers to the Apocrypha.

One passage (Lu 24:44) furnishes clear evidence of the threefold division of the canon. But here again, as in the Prologue of Sirach, there is great uncertainty as to the limits of the 3rd division. Instead of saying "the law, the prophets and the writings," Luke says, "the law, the prophets and the psalms." But it is obvious enough why the Psalms should have been adduced by Jesus in support of His resurrection. It is because they especially testify of Christ: they were, therefore, the most important part of the 3rd division for His immediate purpose, and it may be that they are meant to stand a potiori for the whole of the 3rd division (compare Budde, Encyclopedia Biblica, col. 669).

Another passage (Mt 23:35; compare Lu 11:51) seems to point to the final order and arrangement of the books in the Old Testament canon. It reads: "That upon you may come all the righteous blood shed on the earth, from the blood of Abel the righteous unto the blood of Zachariah son of Barachiah, whom ye slew between the sanctuary and the altar." Now, in order to grasp the bearing of this verse upon the matter in hand, it must be remembered that in the modern arrangement of the Old Testament books in Hebrew, Chronicles stands last; and that the murder of Zachariah is the last recorded instance in this arrangement, being found in 2Ch 24:20-21. But this murder took place under Joash king of Judah, in the 9th century BC. There is another which is chronologically later, namely, that of Uriah son of Shemaiah who was murdered in Jehoiakim's reign in the 7th century BC (Jer 26:23). Accordingly, the argument is this, unless Ch already stood last in Christ's Old Testament, why did He not say, "from the blood of Abel unto the blood of Uriah"? He would then have been speaking chronologically and would have included all the martyrs whose martyrdom is recorded in the Old Testament. But He rather says, "from the blood of Abel unto the blood of Zachariah," as though He were including the whole range of Old Testament Scripture, just as we would say "from Genesis to Malachi." Hence, it is inferred, with some degree of justification also, that Chronicles stood in Christ's time, as it does today in the Hebrew Bible of the Massorets, the last book of an already closed canon. Of course, in answer to this, there is the possible objection that in those early days the Scriptures were still written by the Jews on separate rolls.

Another ground for thinking that the Old Testament canon was closed before the New Testament was written is the numerous citations made in the New Testament from the Old Testament. Every book is quoted except Esther, Ecclesiastes, Canticles, Ezra, Nehemiah, Obadiah, Nahum, and Zephaniah. But these exceptions are not serious. The Twelve Minor Prophets were always treated by the Jews en bloc as one canonical work; hence, if one of the twelve were quoted all were recognized. And the fact that 2Ch 24:20-21 is quoted in Mt 23:35 and Lu 11:51 presupposes also the canonicity of Ezra-Nehemiah, as originally these books were one with Chronicles, though they may possibly have already been divided in Jesus' day. As for Esther, Ecclesiastes, and Canticles, it is easy to see why they are

108

not quoted: they probably failed to furnish New Testament writers material for quotation. The New Testament writers simply had no occasion to make citations from them. What is much more noteworthy, they never quote from the Apocryphal books, though they show an acquaintance with them. Professor Gigot, one of the greatest of Roman Catholic authorities, frankly admits this. In his General Introduction to the Study of the Scriptures, 43, he says: "They never quote them explicitly, it is true, but time and again they borrow expressions and ideas from them." As a matter of fact, New Testament writers felt free to quote from any source; for example, Paul on Mars' Hill cites to the learned Athenians an astronomical work of the Stoic Aratus of Cilicia, or perhaps from a Hymn to Jupiter by Cleanthes of Lycia, when he says, "For we are also his off-spring" (Ac 17:28). And Jude 1:14-15 almost undeniably quotes from Enoch (Jude 1:9; 60:8)--a work which is not recognized as canonical by any except the church of Abyssinia. But in any case, the mere quoting of a book does not canonize it; nor, on the other hand, does failure to quote a book exclude it. Quotation does not necessarily imply sanction; no more than reference to contemporary literature is incompatible with strict views of the canon. Everything depends upon the manner in which the quotation is made. In no case is an Apocryphal book cited by New Testament authors as "Scripture," or as the work of the Holy Spirit. And the force of this statement is not weakened by the fact that the authors of New Testament writings cited the Septuagint instead of the original Hebrew; for, "they are responsible only for the inherent truthfulness of each passage in the form which they actually adopt" (Green, Canon, 145). As a witness, therefore, the New Testament is of paramount importance. For, though it nowhere tells us the exact number of books contained in the Old Testament canon, it gives abundant evidence of the existence already in the 1st century AD of a definite and fixed canon.

9. 4 Esdras (circa 81-96 AD):

4 Esdras in Latin (2 Esdras in English) is a Jewish apocalypse which was written originally in Greek toward the close of the 1st century (circa 81-96 AD). The passage of special interest to us is 2 Esdras 14:19-48 which relates in most fabulous style how Ezra is given spiritual illumination to reproduce the Law which had been burned, and how, at the Divine command, he secludes himself for

a period of 40 days, after which he betakes himself with five skilled scribes to the open country. There, a cup of water is offered him; he drinks, and then dictates to his five amanuenses continuously for 40 days and nights, producing 94 books of which 70 are kept secret and 24 published. The section of supreme importance reads as follows: "And it came to pass, when the forty days were fulfilled, that the Most High spake, saying, `The first that thou hast written, publish openly, that the worthy may read it; but keep the seventy last, that thou mayest deliver them only to such as be wise among the people; for in them is the spring of understanding, the fountain of wisdom, and the stream of knowledge.' And I did so" (4 Esdras 14:45-48). The story is obviously pure fiction. No wonder that a new version of it arose in the 16th century, according to which the canon was completed, not by Ezra alone, but by a company of men known as the Great Synagogue. From the legend of 4 Esdras it is commonly inferred that the 24 books which remain after subtracting 70 from 94 are the canonical books of the Old Testament. If so, then this legend is the first witness we have to the number of books contained in the Old Testament canon. This number corresponds exactly with the usual number of sacred books according to Jewish count, as we saw in section 5 above. The legend, accordingly, is not without value. Even as legend it witnesses to a tradition which existed as early as the 1st Christian century, to the effect that the Jews possessed 24 specially sacred books. It also points to Ezra as the chief factor in the making of Scripture and intimates that the Old Testament canon has long since been virtually closed.

10. Josephus' "Contra Apionem" (circa 100 AD):

Flavius Josephus, the celebrated Jewish historian, was born 37 AD. He was a priest and a Pharisee. About 100 AD, he wrote a controversial treatise, known as Contra Apionem, in defense of the Jews against their assailants, of whom Apion is taken as a leading representative, Now Apion was a famous grammarian, who in his life had been hostile to the Jews. He had died some 50 years before Contra Apionem was written. Josephus wrote in Greek to Greeks. The important passage in his treatise (I, 8) reads as follows: "For it is not the case with us to have vast numbers of books disagreeing and conflicting with one another. We have but twenty-two, containing the history of all time, books that are justly believed in. And of these, five are the books of Moses, which comprise the laws and the earliest traditions from the creation of mankind down to the time of his (Moses') death. This period falls short but by a little of three thousand years. From the death of Moses to the reign of Artaxerxes, king of Persia, the successor of Xerxes, the prophets who succeeded Moses wrote the history of the events that occurred in their own time; in thirteen books. The remaining four documents comprise hymns to God and practical precepts to men. From the days of Artaxerxes to our own time every event has indeed been recorded. But these recent records have not been deemed worthy of equal credit with those which preceded them, because the exact succession of the prophets ceased. But what faith we have placed in our own writings is evident by our conduct; for though so great an interval of time (i.e. since they were written) has now passed, not a soul has ventured either to add, or to remove, or to alter a syllable. But it is instinctive in all Jews at once from their very birth to regard them as commands of God, and to abide by them, and, if need be, willingly to die for them."

The value of this remarkable passage for our study is obviously very great. In the first place Josephus fixes the number of Jewish writings which are recognized as sacred at 22, joining probably Ruth to Jdg and Lam to Jer. He also classifies them according to a threefold division, which is quite peculiar to himself: 5 of Moses, 13 of the prophets, and 4 hymns and maxims for human life. The 5 of Moses were of course the Pentateuch; the 13 of the prophets probably included the 8 regular Nebhi'im plus Daniel, Job, Chronicles, Ezra-Nehemiah, and Esther; the "4 hymns and maxims" would most naturally consist of Psalms, Proverbs, Canticles and Ecclesiastes. There is little doubt that his 22 books are those of our present Hebrew canon.

Another very remarkable fact about Josephus' statement is the standard he gives of canonicity, namely, antiquity; because, as he says, since Artaxerxes' age the succession of prophets had ceased. It was the uniform tradition of Josephus' time that prophetic inspiration had ceased with Malachi (circa 445-432 BC). Hence, according to him, the canon was closed in the reign of Artaxerxes (465-425 BC). He does not pause to give any account of the closing of the canon; he simply assumes it, treating it as unnecessary. Prophecy had ceased, and the canon was accordingly closed; the fact did not require to be officially proclaimed. As remarked above. the value of Josephus as a witness is very great. But just here an important question arises: How literally must we interpret his language? Was the Old Testament canon actually closed before 425 BC? Were not there books and parts of books composed and added to the canon subsequent to his reign? Dr. Green seems to take Josephus literally (Canon, 40, 78). But Josephus is not always reliable in his chronology. For example, in his Antiquities (XI, vi, 13) he dates the story of Esther as occurring in the reign of Artaxerxes I (whereas it belongs to Xerxes' reign), while in the same work (XI, v, 1) he puts Ezra and Nehemiah under Xerxes (whereas they belong to the time of Artaxerxes). On the whole, it seems safer on internal grounds to regard Josephus' statements concerning the antiquity of the Jewish canon as the language not of a careful historian, but of a partisan in debate. Instead of expressing absolute fact in this case, he was reflecting the popular belief of his age. Reduced to its lowest terms, the element of real truth in what he says was simply this, that he voiced a tradition which was at that time universal and undisputed; one, however, which had required a long period, perhaps hundreds of years, to develop. Hence, we conclude that the complete Old Testament canon, numbering 22 books, was no new thing 100 AD.

11. The Councils of Jamnia (90 and 118 AD):

According to the traditions preserved in the Mishna, two councils of Jewish rabbis were held (90 and 118 AD respectively) at Jabne, or Jamnia, not far South of Joppa, on the Mediterranean coast, at which the books of the Old Testament, notably Ecclesiastes and Canticles, were discussed and their canonicity ratified. Rabbi Gamaliel II probably presided. Rabbi Akiba was the chief spirit of the council. What was actually determined by these synods has not been preserved to us accurately, but by many authorities it is thought that the great controversy which had been going on for over a century between the rival Jewish schools of Hillel and Shammai was now brought to a close, and that the canon was formally restricted to our 39 books. Perhaps it is within reason to say that at Jamnia the limits of the Hebrew canon were officially and finally determined by Jewish authority. Not that official sanction created public opinion, however, but rather confirmed it.

12. The Talmud (200-500 AD):

The Talmud consists of two parts: (1) The Mishna (compiled circa 200 AD), a collection of systematized tradition; and (2) the Gemara, Gemara (completed about 500 AD), a "vast and desultory commentary on the Mishna" A Baraitha', or unauthorized gloss, known as the Babha' Bathra' 14 b, a Talmudic tractate, relates the "order" of the various books of the Old Testament and who "wrote" or edited them. But it says nothing of the formation of the canon. To write is not the same as to canonize; though to the later Jews the two ideas were closely akin. As a witness, therefore, this tractate is of little value, except that it confirms the tripartite division and is a good specimen of rabbinic speculation. For the full text of the passage, see Ryle, Canon of the Old Testament, 273 ff.

13. Jewish Doubts in the 2nd Century AD:

During the 2nd century AD, doubts arose in Jewish minds concerning four books, Proverbs, Canticles, Ecclesiastes, and Esther. In a certain Talmudic tractate it is related that an attempt was made to withdraw (ganaz, "conceal," "hide") the Book of Prov on account of contradictions which were found in it (compare 26:4,5), but on deeper investigation it was not withdrawn. In another section of the Talmud, Rabbi Akiba is represented as saying concerning Canticles: "God forbid that any man of Israel should deny that the Song of Songs defileth the hands, for the whole world is not equal to the day in which the Song of Songs was given to Israel. For all Scriptures are holy, but the Song of Songs is the holiest of the holy." Such extravagant language inclines one to feel that real doubt must have existed in the minds of some concerning the book. But the protestations were much stronger against Ecclesiates. In one tractate it is stated: "The wise men desired to hide it because its language was often self-contradictory (compare Ec 7:3 and Ec 2:2;4:2 and Ec 9:4), but they did not hide it because the beginning and the end of it consist of words from the Torah (compare Ec 1:3; 12:13-14)." Likewise Est was vigorously disputed by both the Jerusalem and Babylonian Gemaras, because the name of God was not found in it; but a Rabbi Simeon ben Lakkish (circa 300 AD) defended its canonicity, putting Esther on an equality with the Law and above the Prophets and the other Writings. Other books, for example, Ezekiel and Jonah, were discussed in post-Talmudic writings, but no serious objections were ever raised by the Jews against either. Jonah was really never doubted till the 12th century AD. In the case of no one of these disputed books were there serious doubts; nor did scholastic controversies affect public opinion.

14. Summary and Conclusion:

This brings us to the end of our examination of the witnesses. In our survey we have discovered (1) that the Old Testament says nothing about its canonization, but does emphasize the manner in which the Law was preserved and recognized as authoritative;

(2) that to conclude that the Jews possessed the Law only, when the renegade Manasseh was expelled by Nehemiah from Jerusalem, because the Samaritans admit of the Law alone as the true canon, is unwarrantable; (3) that the Septuagint version as we know it from the Christian manuscripts extant is by no means a sufficient proof that the Alexandrians possessed a "larger" canon which included the Apocrpha; (4) that Jesus ben Sirach is a witness to the fact that the Prophets in his day (180 BC) were not yet acknowledged as canonical; (5) that his grandson in his Prologue is the first witness to the customary tripartite division of Old Testament writings, but does not speak of the 3rd division as though it were already closed; (6) that the Books of Maccabees seem to indicate that Psalms and Daniel are already included in the canon of the Jews; (7) that Philo's testimony is negative, in that he witnesses against the Apocryphal books as an integral part of Holy Scripture; (8) that the New Testament is the most explicit witness of the series, because of the names and titles it ascribes to the Old Testament books which it quotes; (9) that 4 Esdras is the first witness to the number of books in the Old Testament canon-- 24; (10) that Josephus also fixes the number of books, but in arguing for the antiquity of the canon speaks as an advocate, voicing popular tradition, rather than as a scientific historian; (11) that the Councils of Jamnia may, with some ground, be considered the official occasion on which the Jews pronounced upon the limits of their canon; but that (12) doubts existed in the

2nd century concerning certain books; which books, however, were not seriously questioned.

From all this we conclude, that the Law was canonized, or as we would better say, was recognized as authoritative, first, circa 444 BC; that the Prophets were set on an even footing with the Law considerably later, circa 200 BC; and that the Writings received authoritative sanction still later, circa 100 BC. There probably never were three separate canons, but there were three separate classes of writings, which between 450 and 100 BC doubtless stood on different bases, and only gradually became authoritative. There is, therefore, ground for thinking, as suggested above (section 6), that the tripartite division of the Old Testament canon is due to material differences in the contents as well as to chronology.

III. The Canon in the Christian Church.

1. In the Eastern or Oriental Church:

In making the transition from the Jewish to the Christian church, we find the same canon cherished by all. Christians of all sects have always been disposed to accept without question the canon of the Jews. For centuries all branches of the Christian church were practically agreed on the limits set by the Jews, but eventually the western church became divided, some alleging that Christ sanctioned the "larger" canon of Alexandria, including the Apocrypha, while others adhered, as the Jews have always done, to the canon of the Jews in Palestine taking the eastern or oriental church first, the evidence they furnish is as follows: The Peshitta, or Syriac version, dating from circa 150 AD, omits Chronicles; Justin Martyr (164 AD) held to a canon identical with that of the Jews; the Canon of Melito, bishop of Sardis, who (circa 170 AD) made a journey to Palestine in order carefully to investigate the matter, omits Est. His list, which is the first Christian list we have, has been preserved to us by Eusebius in his Eccl. Hist., IV, 26; Origen (died 254 AD), who was educated in Alexandria, and was one of the most learned of the Greek Fathers, also set himself the task of knowing the "Hebrew verity" of the Old Testament text, and gives us a list (also preserved to us by Eusebius, Eccl. Hist., VI, 5) in which he reckons the number of books as 22 (thus agreeing with Josephus). Inadvertently he omits the Twelve Minor Prophets, but this is manifestly an oversight on the part of either a scribe or of Eusebius, as he states the number of books is 22 and then names but 21. The so-called Canon of Laodicea (circa 363 AD) included the canonical books only, rejecting the Apocrypha. Athanasius (died 365 AD) gives a list in which Esther is classed as among the non-canonical books, but he elsewhere admits that "Esther is considered canonical by the Hebrews." However, he included Baruch and the Epistle of Jeremiah with Jeremiah. Amphilochius, bishop of Iconium (circa 380 AD), speaks of Esther as received by some only. Cyril, bishop of Jerusalem (died 386 AD), gives a list corresponding with the Hebrew canon, except that he includes Baruch and the Epistle of Jeremiah. Gregory of Nazianzus in Cappadocia (died 390 AD) omits Esther. But Anastasius, patriarch of Antioch (560 AD), and Leontius of Byzantium (580 AD) both held to the strict Jewish canon of 22 books. The Nestorians generally doubted Esther. This was due doubtless to the influence of Theodore of Mopsuestia (circa 390-457 AD) who disputed the authority of Chronicles, Ezra, Nehemiah, Esther and Job. The oriental churches as a whole, however, never canonized the Apocrypha.

2. In the Western Church:

Between 100 and 400 AD, the New Testament writings became canonical, occupying in the Christian church a place of authority and sacredness equal to those of the Old Testament. The tendency of the period was to receive everything which had been traditionally read in the churches. But the transference of this principle to the Old Testament writings produced great confusion. Usage and theory were often in conflict. A church Father might declare that the Apocryphal books were uninspired and yet quote them as "Scripture," and even introduce them with the accepted formula, "As the Holy Ghost saith." Theologically, they held to a strict canon, homiletically they used a larger one. But even usage was not uniform. 3 and 4 Esdras and the Book of Enoch are sometimes quoted as "Holy Writ," yet the western church never received these books as canonical. The criterion of usage, therefore, is too broad. The theory of the Fathers was gradually forgotten, and the prevalent use of the Septuagint and other versions led to the obliteration of the distinction between the undisputed books of the Hebrew canon and the most popular Apocryphal books; and being often publicly read in the churches they finally received a quasi-canonization.

Tertullian of Carthage (circa 150-230 AD) is the first of the Latin Fathers whose writings have been preserved. He gives the number of Old Testament books as 24, the same as in the Talmud Hilary, bishop of Poitiers in France (350-368 AD), gives a catalogue in which he speaks of "Jeremiah and his epistle," yet his list numbers only 22. Rufinus of Aquileia in Italy (died 410 AD) likewise gives a complete list of 22 books. Jerome also, the learned monk of Bethlehem (died 420 AD), gives the number of canonical books as 22, corresponding to the 22 letters of the Hebrew alphabet, and explains that the five double books (1 and 2 Samuel, 1 and 2 Kings, 1 and 2 Chronicles, Ezra-Nehemiah, Jeremiah-Lamentations) correspond to the five final letters of the Hebrew alphabet. In his famous Prologus Galeatus or "Helmed Preface" to the books of Samuel and Kings, he declares himself for the strict canon of the Jews; rejecting the authority of the deutero-canonical books in the most outspoken manner, even distinguishing carefully the apocryphal additions to Esther and to Daniel. As the celebrated Catholic writer, Dr. Gigot, very frankly allows, "Time and again this illustrious doctor (Jerome) of the Latin church rejects the authority of the deutero-canonical books in the most explicit manner" (General Intro, 56).

Contemporaneous with Jerome in Bethlehem lived Augustine in North Africa (353-430 AD). He was the bishop of Hippo; renowned as thinker, theologian and saint. In the three great Councils of Hippo (393) and Carthage (397 and 419 AD), of which he was the leading spirit, he closed, as it were, the great debate of the previous generations on the subject of how large shall be the Bible. In his essay on Christian Doctrine, he catalogues the books of Scripture, which had been transmitted by the Fathers for public reading in the church, giving their number as 44, with which he says "the authority of the Old Testament is ended." These probably correspond with the present canon of Catholics. But it is not to be supposed that Augustine made no distinction between the proto-canonical and deutero-canonical books. On the contrary, he limited the term "canonical" in its strict sense to the books which are inspired and received by the Jews, and denied that in the support of doctrine the books of Wisdom and Ecclesiasticus were of unquestioned authority, though long custom had entitled them to respect. And when a passage from 2 Maccabees was urged by his opponents in defense of suicide, he rejected their proof by showing that the book was not received into the Hebrew canon to which Christ was witness. At the third Council of Carthage (397 AD), however, a decree was ratified, most probably with his approval, which in effect placed all the canonical and deutero-canonical books on the same level, and in the course of time they actually became considered by some as of equal authority. A few years later, another council at Carthage (419 AD) took the additional step of voting that their own decision concerning the canon should be confirmed by Boniface, the bishop of Rome; accordingly, thereafter, the question of how large the Bible should be became a matter to be settled by authority rather than by criticism.

From the 4th to the 16th century AD the process of gradually widening the limits of the canon continued. Pope Gelasius (492-496 AD) issued a decretal or list in which he included the Old Testament apocrypha. Yet even after this official act of the papacy the sentiment in the western church was divided. Some followed the strict canon of Jerome, while others favored the larger canon of Augustine, without noting his cautions and the distinctions he made between inspired and uninspired writings. Cassiodorus (556 AD) and Isidore of Seville (636 AD) place the lists of Jerome and Augustine side by side without deciding between them. Two bishops of North Africa, Primasius and Junilius (circa 550 AD) reckon 24 books as strictly canonical and explicitly state that the others are not of the same grade. Popular usage, however, was indiscriminate. Outside the Jews there was no sound Hebrew tradition. Accordingly, at the Council of Florence (1442 AD), "Eugenius IV, with the approval of the Fathers of that assembly, declared all the books found in the Latin Bibles then in use to be inspired by the same Holy Spirit, without distinguishing them into two classes or categories" (compare Gigot, General Introduction, 71). Though this bull of Eugenius IV did not deal with the canonicity of the Apocryphal books, it did proclaim their inspiration. Nevertheless, down to the Council of Trent (1546 AD), the Apocryphal books possessed only inferior authority; and when men spoke of canonical Scripture in the strict sense, these were not included.

Luther, the great Saxon Reformer of the 16th century, marks an epoch in the history of the Christian Old Testament canon. In translating the Scriptures into German, he gave the deutero-canonical books an intermediate position between the Old Testament and the New Testament. The Lutheran church, also, while it does not expressly define the limits of the canon, yet places the Apocryphal writings by themselves as distinct and separate from Holy Scripture. This indeed was the attitude of all the early Reformers. In the Zurich Bible of 1529, as in the Genevan version in English of 1560, the Apocryphal books were placed apart with special headings by themselves. Thus the early Reformers did not entirely reject the Apocryphal writings, for it was not an easy task to do so in view of the usage and traditions of centuries.

Rome had vacillated long enough. She realized that something must be done. The Reformers had sided with those who stood by Jerome. She therefore resolved to settle the matter in an ecclesiastical and dogmatic manner. Accordingly the Council of Trent decreed at their fourth sitting (April 8, 1546), that the Apocryphal books were equal in authority and canonical value to the other books of sacred Scripture; and to make this decree effective they added: "If, however, anyone receive not as sacred and canonical the said books entire with all their facts, and as they have been used to be read in the Catholic church, and as they are contained in the Old Latin Vulgate (Jerome's Latin Bible, 390-405 A.D.) edition .... let him be anathema." The decree was the logical outcome of the ever-accumulating snowball tendency in the western church. The historical effect of it upon the church is obvious. It closed forever the field of Biblical study against all free research. Naturally, therefore, the Vatican Council of 1870 not only reiterated the decree but found it easy to take still another step and canonize tradition.

Repeated endeavors were made during the 16th and 17th centuries to have the Apocryphal books removed from the Scriptures. The Synod of Dort (1618-19), Gomarus, Deodatus and others, sought to accomplish it, but failed. The only success achieved was in getting them separated from the truly canonical writings and grouped by themselves, as in the Gallican Confession of 1559, the Anglican Confession of 1562, and the Second Helvetic Confession of 1566. The Puritan Confession went farther, and declared that they were of a purely secular character. The various continental and English versions of the Bible then being made likewise placed them by themselves, apart from the acknowledged books, as a kind of appendix. For example, the Zurich Bible of 1529, the French Bible of 1535, Coverdale's English translation of 1536, Matthew's of 1537, the second edition of the Great Bible, 1540, the Bishops' of 1568, and the King James Version of 1611. The first English version to omit them altogether was an edition of King James' Version published in 1629; but the custom of printing them by themselves, between the Old Testament and the New Testament, continued until 1825, when the Edinburgh Committee of the British and Foreign Bible Society protested that the Society should no longer translate these Apocryphal writings and send them to the heathen. The Society finally yielded and decided to exclude them (May 3, 1827). Since then, Protestants in Great Britain and America have given up the practice of publishing the Apocrypha as a part of sacred Scripture. In Europe, also, since 1850, the tendency has been in the same direction. The Church of England, however, and the American Episcopal church, do not wholly exclude them; certain "readings" being selected from Wisdom, Ecclesiastes and Baruch, and read on week days between October 27 and November 17. Yet, when the English Revised Version appeared in 1885, though it was a special product of the Church of England, there was not so much as a reference to the Apocryphal writings. The Irish church likewise removed them; and the American Standard Revised Version ignores them altogether.

Review Questions

- What is the general meaning of the Greek word biblia?
- How did writers of the Bible testify to its being God's inspired Word?
- What is the Bible canon, and how did this designation originate?
- By when was the canon of the Hebrew Scriptures fixed?
- What are the Apocryphal books?
- How did Josephus and Jerome indicate which books are canonical?
- By when was the canon of the Greek New Testament fixed?

- What has ever been the attitude of the Christian Church toward the Scriptures?

- What two words describe the fact of the recognition of the divine authority of the Scriptures, and the method by which they were so recognized?

- What is the origin and the meaning of these words?

- How did the Books of the New Testament become canonical? When was the first corporate testimony to canonicity given?

- What are the grounds of the canonicity of the Old Testament Books?

- What are the grounds of the canonicity of the New Testament Books?

- What does canonicity involve? To what is it analogous?

- What effect would a failure to canonize the different Books of the Bible have had on their authority?

- Did the revelation of truth come to be because of. canonicity? State the facts of the case.

- What has the Bible sometimes been said to be?

- What was canonization? What was the canonizing process?

CHAPTER 5 Clarity of Scripture

The doctrine of the *clarity of Scripture*[42] (often called the perspicuity of Scripture) is a Protestant Christian position. It teaches that "the infallible rule of interpretation of Scripture, is the Scripture itself; and, therefore, when there is a question about the true and full sense of any scripture (which is not manifold, but one), it may be searched and known by other places that speak more clearly."[43] Clarity of Scripture is an important doctrinal and Biblical interpretive principle for many evangelical Christians. Perspicuity of scripture does not imply that people will receive it for what it is, as many adherents to the doctrine of the perspicuity of scripture accept the Calvinist teaching that man is depraved and needs the illumination of the Holy Spirit in order to see the meaning for what it is. Martin Luther advocated the clearness of scripture in his work *On the Bondage of the Will*.[44] Arminius argued for the perspicuity of scripture by name in "*The Perspicuity Of The Scriptures.*"[45]

This doctrine is in contrast to other Christian positions like that of Augustine,[46] who wrote in *Against the Epistle of Manichaeus* that he "should not believe the gospel except as

---

[42] "All things in Scripture are not alike plain in themselves, nor alike clear unto all; *yet those things which are necessary* to be known, *believed, and observed for salvation*, are so clearly propounded, and opened in some place of Scripture or other, that not only the learned, but the unlearned, in a due use of the ordinary means, may attain unto a sufficient understanding of them [emphasis added]." Kaiser Jr., Walter C.; Silva, Moises (2009-08-12). Introduction to Biblical Hermeneutics: The Search for Meaning (Kindle Locations 4659-4662). Zondervan. Kindle Edition. See paragraph 7 on the doctrine of Scripture in the Westminster Confession of Faith (1647).

[43] Westminster Assembly (1646). "Chapter 1". Westminster Confession of Faith.

[44] Luther, Martin (1931) [1525]. "Erasmus' Scepticism: Section IV". On the Bondage of the Will.

[45] Arminius, Jacobus (1956) [1853]. "The Perspicuity Of The Scriptures". Writings. Grand Rapids, Michigan: Baker Book House.

[46] Mathison, Keith A. (2001). "Augustine". The Shape of Sola Scriptura. Moscow, Idaho: Canon Press. pp. 39–42.

moved by the authority of the Catholic [i.e., universal] Church."[47] And in *On Christian Doctrine*, it says "Let the reader consult the rule of faith which he has gathered from the plainer passages of Scripture, and from the authority of the Church..."[48] Vincent of Lérins concurs, "Therefore, it is very necessary, on account of so great intricacies of such various error, that the rule for the right understanding of the prophets and apostles should be framed in accordance with the standard of Ecclesiastical and Catholic interpretation."[49] The doctrine can also be contrasted by positions, which assert that subjective experience should be preferred over knowing the originally intended meaning of scripture, since it is basically unclear. Finally, the doctrine is contrasted with the more literalist[citation needed] idea that "scientific exegesis" is unnecessary.[50] On this subject Dr. Wayne Grudem writes,

Anyone who has begun to read the Bible seriously will realize that some parts can be understood very easily while other parts seem puzzling. In fact, very early in the history of the church Peter reminded his readers that some parts of Paul's epistles were difficult to understand: "So also our beloved brother Paul wrote to you according to the wisdom given him, speaking of this as he does in all his letters. There are some things in them hard to understand, which the ignorant and unstable twist to their own destruction, as they do the other scriptures" (2 Peter 3:15–16). We

---

[47] Augustine (1890) [397]. "Against the Title of the Epistle of Manichæus". Against the Epistle of Manichæus, Called Fundamental in Philip Schaff, Nicene and Post-Nicene Fathers, Volume IV.

[48] Augustine (1890) [397]. "Rule for Removing Ambiguity by Attending to Punctuation". On Christian Doctrine, Book III. in Philip Schaff, Nicene and Post-Nicene Fathers, Volume II.

[49] Vincent of Lérins (1890) [434]. "A General Rule for distinguishing the Truth of the Catholic Faith from the Falsehood of Heretical Pravity". The Commonitory. in Philip Schaff, Nicene and Post-Nicene Fathers, Volume XI.

Mathison, Keith A. (2001). "The Vincentian Canon". The Shape of Sola Scriptura. Moscow, Idaho: Canon Press. pp. 43–45.

[50] Berkhof, Louis (1996) [1938]. "The Perspicuity of Scripture". Systematic Theology. Grand Rapids, Michigan: William B. Eerdmans Publishing Company. p. 167.

must admit therefore that not all parts of Scripture are able to be understood easily.

But it would be a mistake to think that most of Scripture or Scripture in general is difficult to understand. In fact, the Old Testament and New Testament frequently affirm that Scripture is written in such a way that its teachings are able to be understood by ordinary believers. Even in Peter's statement just quoted, the context is an appeal to the teachings of Paul's letter, which Peter's readers had read and understood (2 Peter 3:15). In fact, Peter assigns some moral blame to those who twist these passages "to their own destruction." And he does not say that there are things impossible to understand, but only difficult to understand.[51]

This author would disagree with Grudem in his suggestion that some parts of scripture is difficult to understand, saying that most of Scripture is not. This author believes it is the other way, most of the Scripture is difficult to understand, and some of Scripture is not.

We are 2,000 years removed from the New Testament books, which were written in Koine ("common") Greek, and there were dozens of cultures, not to mention the idiomatic expressions, metaphors, and so on. We are about 2,400 - 3,500 years removed from the Old Testament books, which were written in Hebrew and Aramaic, makeup dozens of cultures, as well as idiomatic expressions, metaphors, and so on.

There are many rules and principles, which need to be followed in a balanced way if we are to arrive at what the author meant by the words that he used, as should have been understood by his audience. It would be like going to another country, jumping in a car, and start driving without knowing the rules of their roads.

We have 41,000 different varieties of Christianity today, who believe differently. We have tens of thousands of churches in any one given denomination, with each pastor of the same denomination, believing differently. We have a couple billion

---

[51] Grudem, Wayne (2011-02-01). Making Sense of the Bible: One of Seven Parts from Grudem's Systematic Theology (Making Sense of Series) (p. 88). Zondervan.

Christians, who interpret the Bible with no knowledge of how to do so, and carry out *eisegesis* (reading their meaning into the text), not *exegesis* (taking the meaning out of the text).

The Bible is actually very difficult to understand without having a balanced understanding of the interpretive rules. Below are some insights from Dr. Leland Ryken and Dr. Robert H. Stein.

When a Ph.D., like Wayne Grudem, speaks of the Bible as being easy to understand,[52] it is like a person, who has been driving for 20-30 years, telling the new or recently new driver, just how easy it is, forgetting their early days. You have to learn the rules of the road, as well as how to apply those rules in a balanced way, to avoid a fatal crash. The same is true of biblical interpretation rules.[53]

LELAND RYKEN (The Word of God in English)

FALLACY #1: THE BIBLE IS A UNIFORMLY SIMPLE BOOK The drift in modern translations is to produce a colloquial Bible with a simple vocabulary and syntax. What lies behind this drift? Some of the prefaces answer the question. The assumption is that the Bible itself is a simple book intended for people of limited education and intelligence. Here, for example, are statements from prefaces and other documents:

- Since God "stooped to the level of human language to communicate with his people," the translators' task is to

---

[52] Grudem does go on in his chapter to say that parts of the Bible are difficult to understand, but not impossible to understand.

[53] Keep in mind, even if a person has been a Christian for 10, 20, 30-years or more, but has failed to take in the deeper knowledge of things, this means they are still like the new driver, or the new Christian. In other words, they have not learned the rules and principles of biblical interpretation, not to mention many other related areas of study. The apostle Paul spoke of this to the Jewish Christians in Jerusalem,

Hebrews 5:13-6:2 English Standard Version (ESV)

13 for everyone who lives on milk is unskilled in the word of righteousness, since he is a child. 14 But solid food is for the mature, for those who have their powers of discernment trained by constant practice to distinguish good from evil. 6:1 Therefore let us leave the elementary doctrine of Christ and go on to maturity, not laying again a foundation of repentance from dead works and of faith toward God, 2 and of instruction about …

set forth the "truth of the biblical revelation in language that is as clear and simple as possible."'

- "Jesus talked plainly to people.... Jesus, the master Teacher, was very careful not to give people more than they could grasp.... We are trying to re-capture that level of communication.... Jesus was able to communicate clearly, even with children" **(SEB)**.

- "After ascertaining as accurately as possible the meaning of the original, the translators' next task was to express that meaning in a manner and form easily understood by the readers" **(GNB)**

If we take the time to unpack the claims here, the lapses of logic begin to emerge. First, the fact that God stooped to human understanding when he revealed his truth in human words does not itself settle the question of how simple or sophisticated, how transparent or complex, the Bible is. Human language encompasses an immense range of simplicity and difficulty. Nor does the fact that God accommodated himself to human understanding in itself say anything about the level of intelligence and artistic sophistication possessed by the writers and assumed audience of the Bible.

The preface quoted above that cites the example of Jesus to support the claim that the Bible is simple shows how winsome the claims can be on the surface and yet how wrong they actually are when we stop to analyze them. Contrary to the implication of the statement that "Jesus was able to communicate clearly, even to children," we have no recorded statements of Jesus to children. And what about the claim that Jesus "was very careful not to give people more than they could grasp"? This is directly contradicted by Jesus' explanation of why he spoke in parables: "To you [the disciples] it has been given to know ... but to them [the unbelieving masses] it has not been given.... This is why I speak to them in parables, because seeing they do not see, and hearing they do not hear, nor do they understand" (Matthew 13:11, 13, ESV). This is indeed a mysterious statement, already giving the lie to the claim that Jesus' statements are simple and easy to understand. My interpretation of Jesus' statement is that he did not intend his statements to carry all of their meaning on the surface. I would also speak of "delayed action insight" as summing up Jesus' strategy, by which I mean that those who ponder Jesus' sayings will come to an understanding of them, whereas people who are unwilling to penetrate beneath the surface will not.

If we stop to consider what the implied opposites of "simple" are, it becomes obvious that multiple qualities can be set over against simplicity. Something can be simple as opposed to complex and intricate. It can be simple as distinct from sophisticated. Or it can be simple and easy to understand instead of difficult. As we turn now to look at specimens of biblical passages, all of these qualities-simple, complex, difficult, sophisticated-will be present, for the Bible is all of these in different passages.

To test how simple or complex and difficult the Bible is, we need only to look at the text itself. To begin, a cursory glance at any scholarly Bible commentary will reveal at once how difficult a book the Bible often is. Scholars pore over it, write whole books on it, write articles on the minutest details, and disagree with each other (or admit perplexity themselves) over what the text says and means. Even when the vocabulary is translated into simple terms, the very arrangement and content of the material show that the Bible is not a simple book. Consider the following (randomly selected) passage (Isaiah 38:12-13, ESV):

My dwelling is plucked up and removed from me like a shepherd's tent; like a weaver I have rolled up my life; he cuts me off from the loom; from day to night you bring me to an end; I calmed myself until morning; like a lion he breaks all my bones; from day to night you bring me to an end.

This is not a simple passage. It requires one's best powers of concentration to follow the flow of thought and images. In what sense is the speaker's dwelling plucked up? How can a person roll up his or her own life like a weaver? How can God cut a person off from a loom? Exactly how does God bring the speaker to an end? Why does the speaker claim to have calmed himself "until morning," specifically? What does it mean that God brings the speaker to an end "from day to night"? What are we to make of the way in which the speaker shuttles back and forth between referring to God as "he" and "you"? I repeat-this passage is not simple. On the contrary, it is a difficult passage. Let me note in passing that the relative difficulty of the passage is not a matter of vocabulary, and thus merely scaling down the language in translation will not make the passage easy to assimilate.

Related to the claim that the Bible is a simple book is the assumption that the Bible carries all of its meaning on the surface. The passage from Isaiah that I have quoted belies this claim too. One cannot read quickly through the passage. It requires stopping and pondering. This is the normal situation with the Bible, which is a meditative book, often elusive on a first reading.[54]

BELOW IS A SHORT HYPOTHETICAL STORY FROM DR. ROBERT H. STEIN (PP. 11-13)

Tuesday night arrived. Dan and Charlene had invited several of their neighbors to a Bible study, and now they were wondering if anyone would come. Several people had agreed to come, but others had not committed themselves. At 8:00 p.m., beyond all their wildest hopes, everyone who had been invited arrived. After some introductions and neighborhood chit-chat, they all sat down in the living room. Dan explained that he and his wife would like to read through a book of the Bible and discuss the material with the group. He suggested that the book be a Gospel, and, since Mark was the shortest, he recommended it. Everyone agreed, although several said a bit nervously that they really did not know much about the Bible. Dan reassured them that this was all right, for no one present was a "theologian," and they would work together in trying to understand the Bible.

They then went around the room reading Mark 1:1–15 verse by verse. Because of some of the different translations used (the New International Version, the Revised Standard Version, the King James Version, and the Living Bible), Dan sought to reassure all present that although the wording of the various translations might be different, they all meant the same thing. After they finished reading the passage, each person was to think of a brief summary to describe what the passage meant. After thinking for a few minutes, they began to share their thoughts.

---

[54] Leland Ryken. The Word of God in English: Criteria for Excellence in Bible Translation (p. 67-69).

Sally was the first to speak. "What this passage means to me is that everyone needs to be baptized, and I believe that it should be by immersion." John responded, "That's not what I think it means. I think it means that everyone needs to be baptized by the Holy Spirit." Ralph said somewhat timidly, "I am not exactly sure what I should be doing. Should I try to understand what Jesus and John the Baptist meant, or what the passage means to me?" Dan told him that what was important was what the passage meant to him. Encouraged by this, Ralph replied, "Well, what it means to me is that when you really want to meet God you need to go out in the wilderness just as John the Baptist and Jesus did. Life is too busy and hectic. You have to get away and commune with nature. I have a friend who says that to experience God you have to go out in the woods and get in tune with the rocks."

It was Cory who brought the discussion to an abrupt halt. "The Holy Spirit has shown me," he said, "that this passage means that when a person is baptized in the name of Jesus the Holy Spirit will descend upon him like a dove. This is what is called the baptism of the Spirit." Jan replied meekly, "I don't think that's what the meaning is." Cory, however, reassured her that since the Holy Spirit had given him that meaning it must be correct. Jan did not respond to Cory, but it was obvious she did not agree with what he had said. Dan was uncomfortable about the way things were going and sought to resolve the situation. So he said, "Maybe what we are experiencing is an indication of the richness of the Bible. It can mean so many things!"

But does a text of the Bible mean many things? Can a text mean different, even contradictory things? Is there any control over the meaning of biblical texts? Is interpretation controlled by means of individual revelation given by the Holy Spirit? Do the words and grammar control the meaning of the text? If so, what text are we talking about? Is it a particular English translation such as the King James Version or the New International Version? Why not the New Revised Standard Version or the Living Bible? Or why not a German translation such as the Luther Bible? Or should it be the Greek, Hebrew, and Aramaic texts that best reflect what the original authors, such as Isaiah, Paul, and Luke, wrote? And what about the original authors? How are they related to the meaning of the text?

It is obvious that we cannot read the Bible for long before the question arises as to what the Bible "means" and who or what determines that meaning. Neither can we read the Bible without possessing some purpose in reading. In other words, using more technical terminology, everyone who reads the Bible does so with a "hermeneutical" theory in mind. The issue is not whether one has such a theory but whether one's "hermeneutics" is clear or unclear, adequate or inadequate, correct or incorrect.

GRUDEM WRITES: He says that Jesus and the Jews of his day were 1,000, year removed from David, 1,500 years from Moses, and 2,000 years from Abraham, and they did not complain about being centuries removed. (Grudem, Making Sense of the Bible: One of Seven Parts from Grudem's Systematic Theology (Making Sense of Series) 2011, 89)

RESPONSE: This is not completely true, and is misleading. The Jews of that day still lived in a similar kind of custom and culture, as in the days of Abraham, Moses, and David. In fact, it took hundreds of years for styles of clothing to change, unlike today. In addition, they spoke Hebrew-Aramaic and Greek. **Moreover**, they lived by oral evangelism, and it was just 400 years earlier (c. 443 B.C.E.), that they were being taught by Ezra and Nehemiah, inspired authors of the Bible. We could go on and on, as to how they were more in touch with the biblical interpretive rules, not to mention familiarity with the languages, the custom and culture, the idiomatic expressions, the figurative languages and so on. It is a legalistic mindset and greed of wealth and power that got the Jewish teachers off into the weeds of misinterpretation, and the twisting of Scriptures. Let us take a moment below to see how having some understanding of original language words (doing a word study), and Bible backgrounds can enlighten us to what the text means, and how we may apply it in our lives today.

Ephesians 6:12 Updated American Standard Version (UASV)

[12] For our wrestling[55] is not against flesh and blood, but against the rulers, against the powers, against the world-rulers of

---

[55] Or *struggle*

this darkness, against the wicked spirit forces in the heavenly places.

The Greek word for wrestling is *pale*. Do the Greek wrestling matches of Paul's day throw any light on this verse?

Paul shifts the image from warfare to wrestling. Wrestling (*pale*) was a popular event in the games held in Ephesus, Smyrna, Pergamum, and all over Asia Minor. This image communicates more of the directness of the struggle. – *Zondervan Bible Background*, p. 338.

The wrestling match was all about struggling to get the opponent off balance, to throw him to the ground, which would result in a point, and the first to three points, wins.

While the struggles of such wrestling among men, who have herculean strength may seem enough, it should be remembered, these wrestlers had to fight by the rules, which the judges made sure of, "if anyone competes as an athlete, he is not crowned unless he competes according to the rules." – 2 Timothy 2:5, HCSB.

For example, if one wrestler threw another, and the falling man's knee touched the ground, no point was awarded and the judge would punish, by striking him with a stick across the back.

However, unlike the rules strictly implemented above, the unseen enemy that Paul speaks of, he does not live by any rules, as he is a liar, a slanderer, a deceiver, and a murderer. (John 8:44) Therefore, how much more must we struggle against an enemy that has no rules. Therefore, we can understand why Paul would say, 'I weary myself in wrestling ...' – Colossians 1:29, Sadler.

Moreover, when Paul was thrown to the ground, he found strength in his traveling companions, who shared in his obstacles. 'You did well in making yourselves sharers in the fall I got,' (Phil. 4:14 Sadler) *thlipsis* meaning, 'a fall.'

There are times in each Christian life, when one's struggles are beyond our human powers, it could be termed that we suffered from an 'agony of mind.' The Greek, *agnōnia*, meaning a contest, wrestling, struggle, which usually result in much pain. (1 Cor. 9:25) Paul used the term at 1 Tim 6:12, exhorting Christians to "Fight the good fight [struggle your hardest (Weymouth), enter the greatest contest (AT)] of faith."

Jude tells his audience,

Jude 1:3 Updated American Standard Version (UASV)

³ Beloved, while I was making every effort to write you about our common salvation, I found it necessary to write to you appealing that you contend earnestly **[struggling]** for the faith that was once for all delivered to the holy ones.

Jesus said,

Luke 13:24 Updated American Standard Version (UASV)

²⁴ "**Strive [strain every nerve, AT)** to enter through the narrow door; for many, I tell you, will seek to enter and will not be able.

What have we learned thus far? There are times, when a Christian may come into difficult times in the extreme, which may require the struggle of their life. However, it is not hopeless, for God has promised to carry us through what is beyond human strength. The seeking first the kingdom in these moments is what will give us the needed strength, and assure us of a victory, through Jesus Christ,

Romans 8:35-39 Updated American Standard Version (UASV)

³⁵ Who will separate us from the love of Christ? Will tribulation, or distress, or persecution, or famine, or nakedness, or danger, or sword? ³⁶ As it is written,

"On account of you we are being put to death the whole day   long;
    we are considered as sheep to be slaughtered."

³⁷ But in all these things we are more than conquerors through the one having loved us. ³⁸ For I am convinced that neither death, nor life, nor angels, nor rulers, nor things present, nor things to come, nor powers, ³⁹ nor height, nor depth, nor any other created thing, will be able to separate us from the love of God that is in Christ Jesus our Lord.

Walter C. Kaiser Jr. writes,

If all believers are encouraged to use the Bible devotionally, there must be a presumption that the words of Scripture are "perspicuous," that is, clear enough that all can understand what they say without needing the counsel of a scholar at their elbow to instruct them. Is this a reasonable presumption? Can we ensure readers that they will not fall into error when they wander off into the full canon of Scripture, reading the text for themselves, according to their own insights and understandings?

No one was more forceful in taking a stand that the Bible is plain in its meaning and that it should therefore be accessible to all than Martin Luther. His most vigorous affirmation of this principle can be found in his book *On the Bondage of the Will*, written in response to a work entitled *On the Freedom of the Will* by the highly respected scholar Erasmus. According to Erasmus,

> There are some things which God has willed that we should contemplate, as we venerate himself, in mystic silence; and, moreover, there are many passages in the sacred volumes about which many commentators have made guesses, but no one has finally cleared up their obscurity: as the distinction between the divine persons, the conjunction of the divine and human nature in Christ, the unforgivable sin; yet there are other things which God has willed to be most plainly evident, and such are the precepts for the good life. This is the Word of God, which is not to be bought in the highest heaven, not in distant lands overseas, but it is close at hand, in our mouth and in our heart. These truths must be learned by all, but the rest are more properly committed to God, and it is more religious to worship them, being unknown, than to discuss them, being insoluble.[56]

Although Luther at first seemed to disagree violently with Erasmus, implying that everything in Scripture was plain and equally available, he eventually settled down and allowed that there were certain kinds of obscurities in Scripture. "I admit, of course, that there are many texts in the Scriptures that are obscure

---

[56] E. G. Rupp et al., eds., *Luther and Erasmus: Free Will and Salvation*, LCC 17 (Philadelphia: Westminster, 1969), 39–40; emphasis added.

and abstruse, not because of the majesty of their subject matter [as Erasmus had argued], but because of our ignorance of their vocabulary and grammar; but these texts in no way hinder a knowledge of the subject matter of Scripture."[57]

In the end, the argument between Luther and Erasmus was not over the application of learning and scholarship, or even over whether the texts of Scripture were sufficiently clear so that the main message of the Bible could be understood by the average reader. At the bottom of all this debate was this question: To what degree was the average reader, indeed the whole church, obliged to submit to tradition and the official pronouncements of the pope for the proper exposition of Scripture? To this question, the Reformers shouted a loud, "None, for the essential meaning of the message of the Bible!" There was no need of anyone's history of tradition to interpret the Scriptures; the Bible was sufficiently perspicuous without it.

What, then, was meant when the Scriptures were declared to be clear and perspicuous for all? Simply this: the Bible was understood to be clear and perspicuous on all things that were necessary for our salvation and growth in Christ. It was not a claim either that everything in the Bible was equally plain or that there were no mysteries or areas that would not defy one generation of Bible readers or another. If readers would exert the effort one generally put into understanding a literary work, it was asserted that they would gain an understanding that would be adequate and sufficient to guide them into a saving relationship and a life of obedience with their Lord.

The story is told of a woman who approached Mr. D. L. Moody after one of his messages with a complaint. The woman moaned, "Mr. Moody, I can't read the Bible for myself because there are too many things in it I do not understand." Mr. Moody responded, "My good lady, have you ever eaten chicken?" Somewhat annoyed, she replied, "Answer my question first." Moody said, "I am; have you ever eaten chicken?" "Of course, I have," she fired back. "Well, then," Moody continued to press, "What did you do with the bones of the chicken?" "I put them on the side of my plate," she answered with exasperation.

---

[57] Ibid., 110–11.

"Good," Moody commented; "Then do the same thing when you are reading the Bible for yourself. Put any hard things on the side of your plate, because there is still plenty of good eating on the majority of what the Bible has to say."[58] This is not your basic apologetic method, but it does make a strong point.

This definition on the clarity of Scripture was represented in many Protestant works shortly after the Reformation. The best known is paragraph 7 on the doctrine of Scripture in the Westminster Confession of Faith (1647).

All things in Scripture are not alike plain in themselves, nor alike clear unto all; *yet those things which are necessary to be known, believed, and observed for salvation*, are so clearly propounded, and opened in some place of Scripture or other, that not only the learned, but the unlearned, in a due use of the ordinary means, may attain unto a sufficient understanding of them [emphasis added].

More is indeed at stake here than the mere understanding of the words in and of themselves. Even when ordinary laypersons are able to gain an adequate and sufficient understanding of what is being said in the Bible, there is the other dimension of the reception and application of these matters to one's own life and heart. Does this not have an effect on the issue of the clarity of Scripture?[59]

In conclusion, the reason we have so much confusion among the churchgoers and even Christians with an associate, bachelor or Master's degree[60] is that Scripture is difficult to

---

[58] This type of good feeling thinking is more harmful than good. This author has sat in many Bible study classes with churchgoers, who have been consistent and regular at meetings for 10, 20, 30 years, who regularly offered unbiblical answers to Bible study questions. Most of Scripture is complicated and difficult. However, with tools like the one you have in your hands, it can be made easier.

[59] Walter C. Kaiser Jr., "'As the Deer Pants for Streams of Water': The Devotional Use of the Bible," in *Introduction to Biblical Hermeneutics: The Search for Meaning*, ed. Walter C. Kaiser Jr. and Moisés Silva (Grand Rapids, MI: Zondervan, 2007), 215–217.

[60] Many pastors only have a bachelor, meaning they have not taken in the deeper knowledge of things, to be able to pass this on to their congregation. Those who may have a masters, may take a few classes that revolve around

understand for the modern day person. If it were not, we would not have Bible dictionaries and encyclopedias. We would not have a need for Bible handbooks or Study Bibles. We would not need commentaries. We would not need books on Bible backgrounds, or custom and culture books. We would not need word study books. Moreover, most certainly, we would not need the hundreds of books on hermeneutics, exegesis, and biblical interpretation. Some biblical interpretation books are a thousand pages or more.

Let us merely look at *just* the book of Luke and Acts, two Bible books out of sixty-six.

Darrel Bock's Baker Exegetical Commentary on Luke comes in two volumes!

VOLUME 1 Luke 1:1-9:50 is **987 pages**

VOLUME 2 Luke 1:1-9:50 is **1,191 pages**

Totaling **2,178 pages**

Craig S. Keener's Baker Exegetical Commentary of Acts in four volumes

VOLUME 1 Acts: An Exegetical Commentary: Introduction and 1:1-2:47, **1,104 pages**

VOLUME 2 Acts: An Exegetical Commentary: 3:1-14:28, **1,200** pages

VOLUME 3 Acts: An Exegetical Commentary: 15:1-23:35, **1,200 pages**

VOLUME 4 Acts: An Exegetical Commentary: 24:1-28:31, **1,152 pages**

Totaling **4,640 pages**

The Truth Will Set You Free

John 8:31-32 Updated American Standard Version (ASV)

---

interpretation, it is not enough, and many seminaries use books that favor moderate conservative scholarship.

31 So Jesus said to the Jews who had believed him, "If you remain in my word, you are truly my disciples, **32** and you will know the truth, and the truth will set you free.""

Delving into the basics of biblical interpretation, Edward D. Andrews has provided a complete hands-on guide to understanding what the author meant by the words that he used from the conservative grammatical-historical perspective. He teaches how to study the Bible on a deep, scholarly level, yet making it understandable to all. He has sought to provide the very best tool for interpreting the Word of God. This includes clarification of technical terms, answers to every facet of biblical interpretation, and defense of the inerrancy and divine inspiration of Scripture.

Andrews realizes that the importance of digging deeper in our understanding of the Bible, for defending our faith from modern day misguided scholarship. Andrews gives the reader easy and memorable principles and methods to follow for producing an accurate explanation that comes out of, not what many read into the biblical text. The principal procedure within is to define, explain, offer many examples, and give illustrations, to help the reader fully grasp the grammatical-historical approach. Finally, Andrews provides the next generation of Christians, a fresh new Bible reading/study program. This program will not only help the reader know the Bible, but also be able to interpret it, explain it, defend it, and use it when sharing their faith.

Review Questions

- What is the doctrine Clarity of Scripture?

- What is Dr. Wayne Grudem's position on the level of difficulty within Scripture?

- What is the real truth about the level of difficulty within Scripture, and what factors contribute to this?

- What did Grudem say about Jesus and the New Testament persons being 1000 years removed from David, 1500 years removed from Moses, and 2000 years removed from Abraham, and why is that not a reasonable comparison with our being so far removed from Bible times?

Bibliography

Archer, Gleason L. *Encyclopedia of Bible Difficulties.* Grand Rapids: Zondervan, 1982.

Barnett, Paul. *The Birth of Christianity: The First Twenty Years (After Jesus, Vol. 1)* . Grand Rapids, MI: Wm. B. Eerdmans , 2005.

Borgen, Peder. *Philo of Alexandria: An Exegete for His Time.* Leiden, Boston: Brill, 1997.

Brand, Chad, Charles Draper, and England Archie. *Holman Illustrated Bible Dictionary: Revised, Updated and Expanded.* Nashville, TN: Holman, 2003.

Bromiley, Geoffrey W. *The International Standard Bible Encyclopedia (Vol. 1-4).* Grand Rapids, MI: William B. Eerdmans Publishing Co., 1986.

Bruce, F.F. *The Canon of Scripture.* Westmont: IVP Academic, 1988.

Comfort, Philip W. *New Testament Text and Translation Commentary.* Carol Stream: Tyndale House Publishers, 2008.

Deissmann, Adolf. *LIGHT FROM THE ANCIENT EAST: The New Testament Illustrated by Recently Discovered Texts of the Graeco-Roman World.* New York and London: Hodder and Stoughton, 1910.

Elwell, Walter A. *Baker Encyclopedia of the Bible.* Grand Rapids: Baker Book House, 1988.

Ferguson, Everett. *Backgrounds of Early Christianity.* Grand Rapids, MI: Wm. B. Eerdmans, 2003.

Gamble, Henry Y. *Books and Readers in the Early Church: A History of Early Christian Texts.* New Haven: New Haven University Press, 1995.

Geisler, Norman L. *Baker Encyclopedia of Christian Apologetics.* Grand Rapids: Baker Books, 1999.

Grudem, Wayne. *Making Sense of the Bible: One of Seven Parts from Grudem's Systematic Theology (Making Sense of Series)*. Grand Rapids: Zondervan, 2011.

Hill, Charles E., and Michael J. Kruger. *The Early Text of the New Testament*. Oxford: Oxford University Press, 2012.

Johnson, William A, and Holt N Parker. *Ancient Literacies: The Culture of Reading in Greece and Rome*. Oxford: Oxford University Press, 2011.

McKenzie, John L. *Light on the Epistles: A Reader's Guide*. Chicago, IL: Thomas More Press, 1975.

Myers, Allen C. *The Eerdmans Bible Dictionary* . Grand Rapids, Mich: Eerdmans, 1987.

Richards, E. Randolph. *The Secretary in the Letters of Paul*. Tübingen: J.C.B. Mohr, 1990.

Schurer, Emil. *A HISTORY OF THE JEWISH PEOPLE IN THE TIME OF JESUS CHRIST (Volume II)*. Edinburgh: T. & T. Clark, 1890.

Scott, Julius J. Jr. *Jewish Backgrounds of the New Testament*. Grand Rapids, MI: Baker Academic, 1995.

Souter, Alexander. *The Text and Canon of the New Testament*. New York: Charles Scribner's Sons, 1913.

Whiston, William. *The Works of Josephus*. Peabody, MA: Hendrickson, 1987.

www.ingramcontent.com/pod-product-compliance
Lightning Source LLC
LaVergne TN
LVHW041156080426
835511LV00006B/626